A Naturalist's Manor

A Naturalist's Manor

Yan An

Translated by

Chen Du &
Xisheng Chen

chax press
2021

LIBRARY OF CONGRESS CATALOGING-IN-PUBLICATION DATA

NAMES: YAN, AN, 1965- AUTHOR. | DU, CHEN, 1972- TRANSLATOR. | CHEN,
    XISHENG, 1964- TRANSLATOR.
TITLE: A NATURALIST'S MANOR / YAN AN ; TRANSLATED BY CHEN DU & XISHENG
    CHEN.
OTHER TITLES: ZI RAN ZHU YI ZHE DE ZHUANG YUAN. ENGLISH
DESCRIPTION: TUCSON : CHAX PRESS, 2021. | SUMMARY: "A SELECTION OF POEMS
    BY CHINESE POET YAN AN. THE SUBJECTS OF THE POEMS ARE VARIOUS AND
    INCLUDE A BROAD RANGE. THE TRANSLATIONS ARE BY CHINESE TRANSLATORS
    CHEN DU AND XISHENG CHEN"-- PROVIDED BY PUBLISHER.
IDENTIFIERS: LCCN 2021020488 | ISBN 9781946104281 (PAPERBACK)
SUBJECTS: LCSH: YAN, AN, 1965---TRANSLATIONS INTO ENGLISH. | LCGFT:
    POETRY.
CLASSIFICATION: LCC PL2970.5.N2223 Z5 2021 | DDC 895.11/6--DC23
LC RECORD AVAILABLE AT HTTPS://LCCN.LOC.GOV/2021020488

Chax Press / 1517 N Wilmot Rd no. 264 / Tucson AZ / USA
https://chax.org/

Chax is supported by the Arts Foundation of Tucson and Southern Arizona,
and by contributions from individual donors. Chax acknowledges the support
of interns and assistants who contribute to our books. In 2021 our interns and
assistants are David Weiss and Ben Leitner. Our current board of directors
members are Mridul Nanda, Cynthia Miller, Charles Alexander, David Weiss,
Tenney Nathanson, Steven Salmoni, Cole Swensen, and Lauri Scheyer.

We are thankful to all of our contributors and members. Please see http://chax.
org/support-chax-1/ for more information.

I want to dedicate the book to my parents, my sister, and my nephew who have given me unconditional love and helped me rebuild life multiple times. I also want to dedicate the book to all those who have helped me, guided me, and inspired me. — Chen Du

I would like to dedicate the book to my late mother, my father, and my sister who has been taking care of my parents all these years. Also, I am grateful to my best friend Helen and her parents for their generous support to me and my family all these years. Thanks to my good friends Sunny and Zhuomou, and my son Harold. — Xisheng Chen

Contents

I: Ocean Nurturer and the Beauty of Confrontation   13

    The Beauty of Confrontation   15

    Rocks Living in a Yonder Homeland   16

    Naturalist   18

    Quartet: Ocean, Desert, Bottle and Crow   19

    Ocean Observing Journal During the Closed Fishing Season   20

    The Man Digging a Well at the Seashore   21

    Three Objects and Their Relationship With the Horizon   22

    Gong Du Picking Withered Leaves on the Third Statehood
    Lane of Xi'an City   23

    A Few Buddies in the Depths of Mountains by Rivers   25

    Tree of Stars   26

    Six Little Lakes Far in the North   27

    A Far-Reaching Majestic Mountain   28

    The Blue of a Sky-Colored Apron   29

    My Son Running Hither and Thither Under the Starlight   30

    How to Observe Dark Clouds Polish Constellations   31

    Winter of the Old Era and Its Snow Piled Up Like Relics in
    the Outskirts   32

    Chatting About Tea With Five Poets After Drinking Spirits   33

    Direction of Twilight in Ginkgo Manor   35

    A Bare-Handed Lightning Catcher   36

    Tribe of Rocs   37

    He Is Experiencing Dead Branches and Withered Leaves of
    Spring   38

    Owl's Surrealistic Theater   39

    Massive Boulders Rolling in the Depths of the Yellow River   41

    Stray at the Littoral National Seagull Park   43

    The Spring of River, Crow and Plastic Bag   45

    A Tree Blacklisted by a Felling Company   46

    Dark Tempest of Last Year   47

    Observer of the Egg of the World   48

    Today Your Soul Should Choose to Sail in the Ocean   49

    Gripping Stars at a Maritime Museum   51

    Oral Narrative of an Ocean Nurturer   52

The Qin Mountains   53

Moorland Is My Friend   54

Nest of the Tenebrosity   55

Kua Fu Chasing Clay Balls in the Park   56

II: *Dangerous Nests of the Dream Clinic*   57

Holding My Tongue at the Subway All Day Long   59

Earth Is a Balloon With a Pain in Its Heart   61

The World and Its Dangerous Nests   63

Fish-Eating Man and Potato-Eating Man   64

Writing Lyrics for a Rocker at a Subway Passage   65

Letters to the Clouds   66

Grey Overcast Sky Above the Bell Tower   67

A Man's Knife Glint, Moonlight and Starshine   68

Three Poets or the Most Melancholy One   69

An Aesthete's Nails and Hammer   70

A Man With a Horrible Dent in His Head   71

Cliff With Cranes   72

Falling White Snow and Blooming Red Plum Blossoms   73

Aborted Visit to the Yellow River in the Central Plains   74

A Narrow Escape From a Breathtaking Encounter at an Ancient
Ferry on the Yellow River   75

Spring Rain and Mist of the Central Plains   77

Going Northwards, at the Height of a Bird   79

Black and White in the Bright Blue Sky   80

Blank and Melancholy   81

Blue Boy Smuggling Birds' Nests up the Trees   82

Dream Clinic in a Mirror   83

Nobody Can See the Shattering of an Angelic Lady's Heart   85

By the Ocean   86

Between Ocean and Revolution   87

Three Maidens and Belated-Blooming Northern Cherry Blossoms   88

Spring and Fairness   89

Fluttering Leaves in Lonesome Northern Winter   90

City and Its Underground Worker   91

Scene at Dusk   92

The Man Cutting Down Trees   93

The Mediterranean Sea   95

Different Forms of Mourning   96

Humble Sea-Watcher   97

The Reason I Like Glass   98

III: All the World's Birds Are Flying Towards Twilight   99

All the World's Birds Are Flying Towards Twilight   101

On a Sinner-Like Wasteland   102

Observation of a Flying Flamingo   103

Curved Scenery   104

Firmament by the Bell Tower   105

Marmot Singing in the Morning Glow   106

Mary's Blizzard and Boy   107

Python of Time   108

Portrait: Sketch of Another Tree   109

A Fish Controlled by an Accidental Ideal   110

Heavier or Lighter: Fall of Butterfly or Airplane   113

Fruits Flying Towards All Corners of the World Like Birds   114

Leaves Fluttering Down Profusely Under the Starry Sky   116

The Man Always Walking Ahead   117

Woman in Exotic Dress   119

Peace-Minded Man by the Salween River   121

Ennui   122

Horizon Bent by Gloomy Clouds Part I   123

Horizon Bent by Gloomy Clouds Part II   125

History of Clouds   128

Red Fox: A Legend   129

Four Birds at the Watershed Between the River and the Ocean   130

A Girl Talking With a Mirror   131

Porcelain Cleaner in a Gloomy Apartment   132

Talking About Snow With a Girl in a Café   133

Man With a Nose As Huge as a Spacecraft   134

The Place I Want to Go   135

Seven Lakes and Seven Swans   136

Reasons for Only Reading Friends' Books   137

Demise of the Starry Sky   138

Men Bringing Stones From Afar   139

I

Ocean Nurturer and the
Beauty of Confrontation

The Beauty of Confrontation

I am not a simple naturalist
That is to say I am not a bee   or a river
Or a man taking advantage of anthesis or floodtime
To get close to the nearly crumbled goals of the world
I am a man holding fast to an iron pickaxe
Holding fast to a fistful of shattered glass
Holding fast to an iron pickaxe that gleams due to overuse
Walking, on and off   always selecting and surveying the land
Always excavating the earth and its yonder silence
I spread a fistful of shattered glass
On an old courtyard and a desolate region
As if I were scattering a fistful of seeds on an unidentified star

I dig in the sandy land unploughed by earthworms
I dig in alkali soils uncorroded by tree roots
I dig in a beach wasteland lapped up by waves
Under the starry sky   at the place where the darkness
Renders the world more profound and unfathomable
Sometimes when I lose the patience to excavate
I spread shattered glass as if I were scattering a fistful of seeds

Eventually   I dig in myself
Inside my body   in a zone where life and death
Secretly accommodate with each other
I dig out another starry sky
And the bizarre debris and waste that belong to it
Those shards as tameless as shattered glass
All for nothing   but to witness in person
What is between them and the galaxy above my head
The rapport as hard to elucidate as a wad of cotton
Or the beauty of confrontation

Rocks Living in a Yonder Homeland

You should retreat   in the yonder of Homeland
You should retreat into the depths of the land like a hermit
To take a look at the rocks having transformed time into odds and ends
That are plugged into the sandy land topsy-turvy
Or secluded in a remote area in Northern China
Or the luxuriant woods in the South
By the form of an entire mountain   or the lofty bluffs of an ancient valley

It is the rocks that come earlier than a wolf and a grove of trees
And guard the hills and valleys
Just like messengers inside time

After the wolf and trees
Are gnawed away into nihility piece by piece by a silent wind
The rocks are still holding firm in the moors and desolation
Their thirst is as deep as that of a desert
As deep as an abandoned well
And, like a tent
Completely dilapidated on a sand dune
Or the bank of a lake whence a dinosaur has grabbed a drink
With nowhere to hide

Those rocks are smuggled from the universe
By silent winds and torrents higher than rivers
Sometimes they travel with the currents   but more often
They like to dwell in a primitive zone
Where people haven't found a chance to move the boulders for
          other purposes
Indifferent to the river running afar on its own
Or disappearing into the yonder like a somnambulist

Like a grim bird of time
Solidifying its dream to fly on the heart of time
The rocks living in a yonder homeland

Retreat   retreat like a hermit
Your trip won't disappoint you   you will meet them unexpectedly

Naturalist

If I want to write about a rebar piercing through the chest of a
        construction worker
I will write about magma and the secret air holes deeply inside its
        internal flames

If I want to write about the cities and building complexes, both of which
        grow like monsters
I will write about unnamed mountains and the heavenly dog above them
        that swallows the moon like a pancake

If I want to write about vehicle emissions and smog
I will write about the bulls in the old society defecating in a village after
        eating too many poppies

If I want to write about a dumping ground filled with shattered glass,
        used leather and plastic waste
I will write about a man having swallowed arsenic and a steelyard weight
And lying dead in the moors with hands and legs in the air like a crow

Quartet: Ocean, Desert, Bottle and Crow

At the ocean, subconsciously holding fast to my parochialism
I scooped up seawater as if I were retrieving a dead body
I put the water in a bottle once containing sulfuric acid
Shook the bottle again and again   as if it were a colossal ship sailing
        in a hurricane
And shaking my heart and the watchtower on the mast

In the vast desert   I was a man pouring out the seawater from the bottle
A man looking for seawater like searching for a lost person
A man having to put in the bottle the desert moistened by the seawater
I ceaselessly shook the bottle   to precipitate out the spring water
However when carelessly sleeping on the bottle as a pillow
I dreamt of a sandstorm raging over the ocean
And the white neck of a whale unfortunately stuck on the bottleneck

On a lofty mountain, I was a swan watcher
A man filling the bottle with snow just like pearls
A man bumping into a crow   and discussing with it the issue of
        drinking water
When the crow told me that the water-drinking issue
Was actually an issue about the ocean, about the desert, and about myself
Eventually I became a man confined by the swan's flight and shadow
On top of a mountain and hurling stones for no reasons

Ocean Observing Journal During the Closed Fishing Season

The firmament and meteorites have fed the appetite of the ocean
The lighthouse has ceased   to shine upon the ocean
That seems to broaden the vision
Of a spectator at the highest seashore
Whales are practicing   among the stars
Rising and setting like isles
Whilst the ocean is exercising quietude in the depths of heavy mists

Whether you flint stones into the ocean
Or dump water into the ocean
Or cast the image of sunrise and moonset into the ocean
The ocean accepts all with delight
So are the stars and white clouds in the ocean

The ocean, like a gigantic bird's nest
Embraces a bottomless abyss and blue
Incubated inside the blue are boulders   whales
The density and piercing cold of lightning
And volcanoes converging their own ashes

The ocean is an enormous ridiculous blue bird
With the world in the hearts of its islands and starry sky
Just like deep sea fish during the closed fishing season
Gradually emerging from the depths of near nihility
Towards the visible obviousness

The Man Digging a Well at the Seashore

The man digging a well at the seashore
Looks wan   and gloomy
He is familiar with the headland, dull seabirds and even sea ghosts
Sometimes he lives with them in the mountains
Sometimes he lives alone on a reef
Sometimes he lives, when the fishing season is over
On a tottering mast whence he can overlook the entire ocean

The ocean is like a sapphire blue wasteland
Surrounded by white spindrifts and mournful warbles of white seabirds
All the white birds are still soaring above the ocean
All the black birds are winging in the sky
The man digging a well at the seashore
Is like a gigantic spider   using a fishing net
To suspend himself from the teetering mast

Like a seabird with wings broken many times by the ocean
The man digging a well at the seashore
Knows very well secrets of the ocean
His small well is so exquisite
So crystal clear   that all the people coming to watch the ocean want
            to drink from it
A fish conceiving for long but unable to spawn wants to drink from it
Even the entire ocean dying of thirst
Wants to drink from it

Three Objects and Their Relationship With the Horizon

Three objects are crossing the horizon at the same time
An ant
A marmot
A man with the facial expression of old steel or embers

The ant is pursuing clouds
The marmot is chasing after the wilderness
The man is running after the horizon

However the one who can surpass the ant and the marmot
And forge ahead towards the next horizon
Is still that man
He is closer and closer to a vast expanse of grassland
And is closer and closer to the starry sky

Gong Du Picking Withered Leaves on the Third Statehood Lane of Xi'an City

He picks cobwebs secretly shrouding the depths of the garden tree crowns
And scraps of paper adhering to wall corners like fallen leaves
But deliberately leaves alone the dust at the minutest places
"Dust is a time-related matter
With nobleness contained in lowliness
Only a fine nurturing heart
Can perceive its hidden auspiciousness"
He picks the dead leaves on money trees
Full of rusty spots   completely withered leaves one after another
He has exploited his embroidery skills to carefully pick the leaves
And has even utilized a pair of scissors   to cut off
Several twigs teeming with perished leaves
He said: do not cultivate dust on the windows
Keep yourself too busy   or always keep your nose to the grindstone
Find time to look out the window   and count
The oriental plane trees on Statehood Road and the lane
With leaves as big as hardy banana leaves calling for gaze
The solitude of the firmament, above the plants, with no flying birds
And the starry sky, at night, with looming pearls and starshine
Incalculable as they are, keep counting

The trees on Statehood Road and the lane   hinder the city's
Increasingly heavy traffic and the routing of more overhead power lines
So each year, some are sawed off or cut down
Leaves damaged by scorching weather and insect pests
Leaves with veins disconnected by knives, axes and saws
Leaves broken by autumn gales
Which are the most   which are the least
Call for the man who records the density of teardrops
To establish a record of the statistics

Gong Du said our trees will be less and less
There aren't a lot of shriveled leaves yet

Pick while you can
It is a bliss to be able to pick

A Few Buddies in the Depths of Mountains by Rivers

The few good buddies into the mountains by rivers
Each are a foresightful and farsighted man
Whose industriousness and wisdom are more than sufficient
The dried-up well in the mountains has no way to stump them
The water in their kettles is sufficient for their lifetime
A chunk of ice unmelted in summer by a fluke
With condensed clouds, mists and the sharpness of sunset
Is way enough for their lifelong enjoyment

Among the few good buddies into the mountains by rivers
Are Li Bai, Wang Wei, and Xuanzang in a brown linen garment
Along with chrysanthemums and pines   a phoenix and an eagle
And coldwater fish   silent fish
Submerged in the depths of a deep pool more deeply than stones
The few good buddies of mine   good buddies
Have an unfettered and eventful life
They sweep fallen leaves and sunset on a cliff
Drink spirits, sip tea and listen to the wind in the moonlight
And watch the silent fish float from the bowels of the deep pond
One by one   and scratch the water surface in the dark
With susurration as subtle as a wind caressing a grassland

The few good buddies into the mountains by rivers
Are living in an era not far away
They grow crops without weeding   plant trees other than flowers
To my untimely and inopportune visit
They react with a mere peep from behind leaves
I am going to chase after the zephyr in the valley
Shake down pine nuts all over the ground
And a treeful of white lilac blossoms
Shinier than the bright moonlight
And slowly inquire about their whereabouts

Tree of Stars

With its relocation from afar
This towering tree has brought a lake
A water well
An ocean and its azure blue
And the endless vastness
That can almost contain the entire starry sky

She is seeking beneath the thickest earth in the universe
The roots that belong or don't belong to her
Amongst the stars   she stares up at her heart-shaped branches
Green leaves and constellation-like fruits
As well as the nest that can house
Not only flying birds but fruitage and time

The tree of stars   is breathing between the earth and stars
Has planted, among God, soil and stalactites
The cool umbrage of plane trees and oriental cherry blossoms
And is playing, between love and the pattering rain
The bowstring-like undulation of the earth
And also the dreamland more enchanting than the horizon
Only the earth is entitled to have

The tree of stars   only from the magnificent Qin Mountains
From a majestic river   from the moon
And from the vast wilderness can one catch a delightful glimpse of her
How much incalculable growth
And how much immeasurable height does she need
So that she can incubate in her nest
The twinkling stars like eggs of dreams

Neither you nor I know the answer
Only heaven knows

Six Little Lakes Far in the North

Six little lakes far in the North
Six little crystal clear, translucent dews
Live on a plateau barely with flying birds
A plateau rarely with cursorial animals
And in the hearts of the horizon and northern grassland
Wearing a grass apron
And caressing skin-to-skin with the sky all day long

On the banks of the six little lakes
Miserable giant boulders are piled up on Mongolian cairns
Birds and beasts with superior lung capacities
Rush towards here   like successive surging waves
With lots of them dying on the road one by one
The mournful stone mounds   slate grey stone mounds
Are residences of their white sleek furs and souls

The six little lakes   are little ones of deities
That can never be drained by little animals
They are clean and beautiful   besides water
There are still water
And free mosquitoes and flies clustering around the water

The six little lakes   the lakes of deities
Are hidden like pearls inside the heart of the universe
Only Pegasus and swans
Only a spirit beast as mysterious as a kylin
Only an angel knows how to sip from them

A Far-Reaching Majestic Mountain

The mountain majestic for its far-reachingness other than loftiness
Its exploration is just like a grope for secrets
Or a dangling rope linking two bluffs over a valley
Which is dangerous

Just like a dive off a cliff
And a cry for help with the fall chasing the dream of the fall
In the far-reaching yet majestic mountain
With white clouds overhead
Its birds behave like lonely mavericks on white clouds
And never fly close to the ground
Inside its woods live monsters
Its meadows   are luxuriant in some years
But raged by yellow gales and locusts in others
Slowly exposing a desolate open space
The destitute yet unadulterated brook currents
Are not as enormous as before   but still laving boulders
As well as the internally encapsulated
Wretched yet implicit white

The mountain majestic for its far-reachingness other than loftiness
Its meandering paths are so much like curves   or ropes
That they have garroted many travelers
Tigers   lions   and men picking pearls from volcanic ashes
I have prepared for years   will cross it as well
And will be trapped into its rope-like curves as well
Like the sun setting behind the mountains
(If it can be regarded as death)
It is worth dying for

The Blue of a Sky-Colored Apron

The woman scything grass and the sun in the mountains for a lifetime
Cutting grass to feed livestock   mowing the sun to feed us
Coloring fabric with plant liquids and sewing clothes for us
Washing decayed wood and grime in the Yellow River
Carrying a jar of water for Father and the scorching sun on the mountaintop
Dyeing white cloth black, blue, red or green
And then heavily decorating the bleak era of desolation
Uttering her children's pet names in her entire life but forgetting to sing
At a place with the sky bluer than the blue of a sky-colored apron
Atop the mountain, watching a flock of birds and the sun fall behind
          boundless mountains
Last year I returned to my hometown   and planted some grass on her grave
This year I returned to my hometown   and planted some trees on her grave
I will return to my hometown again next year
To dye again the sky and the blue of her sky-colored apron
With the technique she invented to color white cloth when she was alive
Gingerly and cautiously

Mother   heaven is too far   the mortal world is even farther
However our teardrops   corpses and ashes
Will be scattered on or aggregated by a strange land like windblown dust
Someday in the future   the blue of your sky-colored apron
Will too be laden with windblown dust and dead twigs
The walls and firmament you left behind
Will no longer be dyed by anyone   will gradually fade to white
As white as having nothing at all
Really nothing at all

My Son Running Hither and Thither Under the Starlight

My son's territory is in the wild mountains
He is a bear hunter
Chasing after each other with a bear or an ursidae animal
And traveling alone through a deeply secluded valley like a wild beast
My son is running hither and thither under the starlight

He cuts his way through exuberant straggly bushes to salvage a trapped wolf
Exploiting the wolf's difficulties   he even brings it home multiple times
My son has planted rifles on a barren mountain as if they were trees
And planted knives in the howling of wolves and the night sky
As a brilliant hunter keeping company with the mountains
Keeping company with everything
And honing himself by dipping into the starlight
He only shoots with arrowheads made of twigs
Fires with bullets made of wood
And uses a both giant and hollow, empty bird's nest
To harvest the heavenly music and mercy under the starry sky

With clay ramparts   tough stones and thorn hedges
He accommodates the river entrenched in a valley, and its soul
And raises his wounded plant-like palm
Up into the starry sky as if he were growing or uplifting it
As if he were enduring   the stars after incineration at night
Like injured birds
Returning to the thickets under the starry sky
Returning to the nest vacated over time
And filled with dense fine dust and quietude

How to Observe Dark Clouds Polishing Constellations

You must be like a flying saucer
In either the dark or the translucent universe
Roving like an uncontrolled leaf
And gliding like an unrestrained spider
Only then can you have the privilege of witnessing occasionally
Dark clouds wipe the dimness from the constellations

You must cultivate yourself into a sprite or nix at the world's end
Be truly familiar with the changed direction of a mountain range
And the peacefully secluded place even monsters can't reach
Only then can you have the fortune to observe sporadically
How dark clouds wipe the gloom from the constellations

You must be a meteorite having voluntarily stopped plummeting
Or a bird that thoroughly comprehends how to fly in the universe
And must be able to arbitrarily open or close, in nihility
Warehouses, from space shuttles, for piling up debris and waste
Once in a while   as it is so peaceful and quiet
You may see dark clouds clearing the obscurity of the constellations

The feathery clouds among the stars   are like the water in an abyss
Solitarily flowing towards a deeper abyss
As if it were infusing nonexistence
If you have the privilege of witnessing with your own eyes
Then you are lucky enough to experience in person
Dark clouds repeatedly polishing the murkiness of the constellations

Winter of the Old Era and Its Snow Piled Up Like Relics in the Outskirts

A sleepyhead belonging to the summer of the old era
Hasn't literally or formally woken up
The winter with snowbound mountains is about to come
He hasn't paid a visit to the outskirts with a frozen river and moors
Or experienced the paths turning grayish due to blowing gales and
      fallen leaves
Or snooped around on rabbits and wolves
That have carried home many gifts rolled in dust
And then have lain in wait in a concealed position like spiders
An abrupt and unexpected snowstorm has ushered the entire universe
To a slumber as heavy as that of an old grizzly bear

The sleepyhead belonging to the summer of the old era
Wakes up in a blizzard never heard of before
Like a trapped beast with costae painfully stabbed by a falchion like
      a cold blast
Having been cornered   he revolves in the patio
Ceaselessly hones a knife on a rough tough stone in an old castle
Gradually discerns the fine slivers of light on the entire blade
Meanwhile catches clearly   on the somber saturnine eave
A cobweb hanging from last year   more little spiders hidden and lurking
Inside the empty spider shell
The old web used this summer and the new web to be launched next year
And seven ignited gigantic candles
In place of a giant timepiece and a colossal chandelier

A heavy snowfall in the winter of an old era
Like a heap of vintage books   or a stack of undeliverable letters
Are piled up like relics under the cliff in the outskirts
By then the sleepyhead of summer has awakened
Has heard all the tidings about winter
His sadness and lament is like a hibernating serpent
That breaks free of an occupied and wreathed dreamland
And gradually comes awake

Chatting About Tea With Five Poets After Drinking Spirits

With lip contours more precisely clear-cut than a sculpture's
Mr. Li Yan, fond of gentility and linguistic art, drew an analogy:
Spirits is for the North   tea for the South
Tea is green and spirits white
It is more than a matter of color
Tea can tranquilize the mind   spirits foresees providence
It is neither an issue of whether they are produced in the South or the North
Nor an issue of the layout of lightness and heaviness
It is just like penicillin desiring to live in the earth, rocks, seawater
And their inflammation as subtle yet lethal as bacteria

Mr. Yan An, a master of sorcery and astrology, hugging a glass jar
Was shaking the psychic clay he had cultured for years   from beach
       sand dunes
He proposed an explanation tinted with witchcraft and animism:
Tea is a messenger from the realm of plants
Aided by water's strength, it continuously regresses us to grass and leaves
As to spirits   a compulsory, tolerant and dispirited fire-taking method
Resurrected with your appetite and blood vessels
Its flames will eradicate your lifeblood
Its blaze will also engulf your brain
As if it were hollowing out your body   men of integrity and wisdom
Should know when enough is enough

Mr. Zong Tingfeng, with upside-down-clock sleep disorder
Liked to be quiet like water   however was struck by a whim:
How about water   which is more influential to the world than tea
       and spirits
Look, how many amazing fish are cultivated in there
Hideous but still adorable fish   white, black and red-mottled fish
Maybe there is a crocodile lurking in farther depths
Oh, how about the horse having gone afar and carried water for a lifetime
Or maybe I should sing a nursery rhyme I almost forget
——Eat horsemeat   have fish soup
    No water, nothing can be done

With pupils bluer than the azure sky and the blue ink of the Aegean Sea
Mr. Gao Hong, fond of solo contemplation like a monster
Got in such a mood that he rushed to yell:
The best way is to find the carpenter I know
To borrow a ruler from him (the one I once used)
Or to find the blacksmith I was acquainted with before
To borrow his iron hammer (with which I once smashed an ox to death)
I would measure with the ruler the distance travelled by a fish and a camel
And the duration from birth to death in water of a bottle of liquor and a
            kettle of tea
I want to try hammering the lake frozen with ice
Ask it how many tons of blue and salt are loaded in its belly
And how the swans full with lake water can accompany a steamer
While flying ceaselessly over the Pacific, the Indian Ocean or the Atlantic

Mr. Jia Qin seemed reluctant to participate in the discussion   in a trance
He wrote on the back of a piece of cigarette wrapper:
Actually both tea and spirits are water of wisdom and truth
Inside each pot of tea soundly sleep deities and angels   we've missed for long
Inside each jar of aged liquor a broadsword is forged   as well as earthenware
Iron and damp gunpowder too much to fill in a big barrel
Marine vessels and compasses in the fierce ocean
We've missed for long

Five poets satiated with spirits other than food under the grey lake-colored
            starry northern sky
Expatiated on diverse profound topics at the border of gravida-like
            sand dunes
I sat among them like a bystander
In the late night's heavy darkness with dim starlight

Direction of Twilight in Ginkgo Manor

A wind has altered the twilight's direction
And also the direction of the darkness perching on the trees
Just like the fruits on ginkgo trees and their unripe odor
Just like the leaves prematurely withered by encroaching of green caterpillars
Today it is from above that darkness
Is plummeting straight down

The wind has altered the twilight's direction
And also the direction of the darkness dwelling on the trees
Darkness is like gloomy starshine
And a black bird chasing after descending fruits
Today it alights from above
And from the dense umbrage of trees

Just like doomed catastrophic comets
Also accompanied by fall of darkness and giant early-withered leaves are
Sharp prickles and pains   some kind of itchiness sheerly like ulceration's
The prickles and pains that require one to mobilize the entire night
Or to alert an emergency physician of a traumatology hospital
To restrain or bandage

From a park with no warning signs of plant diseases and insect pests
From above a middle-aged man strolling alone in the dusky park
Just like some omenless internal strike
Just like doomed catastrophic comets
They all plummet straightforwardly

A Bare-Handed Lightning Catcher

Many friends are destined to leave
Many things are doomed to vanish
Just like we are bound to see dust and cinders
Just like cloud shadows and broad-leaved epiphyllums

Just like a bare-handed lightning catcher
Just like the grey bristles and manes of wolves
Running hither and thither on a moorland
Running hither and thither on the mountain ridges
Just like some kind of hallucination flashing by
In the bleak twilight or broad daylight
Just like stones, falling with a waterfall
That glitter-glister in the splashing white light of the falls
The bare-handed lightning catcher
Many trees have been knocked down by him
Many mountains have been overthrown by him
Many rivers have been held in his hands like handles
As if he were holding whips

The man who lashes us with a whip
Who thrashes trees, hills and dales
Who slashes top-heavy hairy savages
Who catches lightning with bare hands
Is the man who is waiting for us
To catch our own and the world's
Ghost shades and silhouettes
As if we were hunting bears in shadows

Tribe of Rocs

The tribe of rocs is living in the depths of the ocean
Or a world deeper and farther than the ocean's bowels
With no human being ever born
But with many gigantic birds   and a lot of small birds
A place accessible to no voyage
Except for those from the tribe of supergiant rocs
No birds   including those larger than rocs
And known as spaceships
Can fly over the place

A jumbo timber from the tribe   becomes a titanic ship when floating on
        the ocean
How the colossal timber vessel drifts playfully on the sea
How it hops and drops shattering the anonymous ocean
How the cracked ocean soars to pursue dark clouds
And the festering-like blue of the sky and seawater behind the dark clouds
And then produces a tribe of rocs, similar to yet larger than a convocation
        of eagles
And enables the rocs to fly back to the tribe reachable by neither humans
        nor birds
All of these are part of the daily life and everyday games
Of the giant birds of the tribe of rocs

The beauty of the lonely yet magnificent mysterious territory of the tribe
        of rocs
Lies in an abyss full of falls and flights   with endless throughput capacity
Like a python engulfing a mammoth at the depths of a prehistoric wilderness
And when fully sated, starting to sip the ocean with the soaked moon
As if lethal nihility were going to gradually ingest everything
The ocean will slowly sink at its depths   the whole world
Including the unknown tribe of rocs
And the world, delineated by navigators and beacons
Where the known and the unknown are inseparably entangled
Will also gradually sink in there

He Is Experiencing Dead Branches and Withered Leaves of Spring

On the Statehood Road of Xi'an City
The withered plane tree leaves from last winter
Are still lingering on the trees
And remain all the time until this spring

Last winter witnessed no snow
It was a mild warm season
The plane trees of last winter
In a whirl of gale of this spring
In languid rustles, shed
Their own dead branches and withered leaves

A man having experienced the dead branches and withered leaves of autumn
And undergone the dead branches and withered leaves of winter
Is a lynx-eyed man
The first to see the fallen leaves of spring

A man ceaselessly chasing after and counting the leaves
A man endlessly treading and jumping on the leaves
A man continuously driving away sanitation workers
For arbitrary possession of all the fallen leaves in spring

A man claiming it's dangerous to sweep fallen leaves in spring
And embracing fallen leaves like pets in arms

Owl's Surrealistic Theater

I am a bird living on the treetops
On the acme of clouds
And on the tips of snow and flames

I am a bird having lodged a pebble
(Sometimes a handful of debris from a disintegrated rocket)
In the throat of the sun as if it were a fishbone
Causing the sun to cough incessantly   devour smog ceaselessly
Until it has engulfed a great deal of dust and ashes
And thereby is gradually losing vision
And can only see the dust and ashes

I am a bird having mistakenly swallowed time
I keep excreting stones, flames and meteorites
And end up with a poor reputation

I am a bird dwelling in a nest made of dead branches and iron wires
With a head looking like a monster's
Feathers resembling fish scales
Wings similar to not only thunders and lightning but also broken trees
And looking like a fledgling in a nightmare
Waiting for the nightmare to be alleviated
Or exterminated

I am a bird who attacks kites and airplanes from time to time
Enables them to disappear secretly from the world
And thereby becomes a legend of the genesis of the world

I am a bird having built its nest in a shadow as unreachable as imaginary
Having constructed its nest in flames and a dreamland
And having mounted its nest, as if it were flames or a dreamland
Onto the centers of destruction and bluffs
In an attempt to accomplish extreme flights

My nest is half of the world and its heart
My flights are the ominous cries and silence
Of an unformed infant on the bloody tree crotch
I will crack with my beak the world's massive boulders
With hidden sinister motives and concealed nightmares and reveries
Until the slurry and souls of stars spill over

I am a bird with a poor reputation
A ferocious bird   with an indescribable habitat
Who is more difficult to control
Than stars and meteorites

I am a bird more difficult to control
Than kites   cotton   menstruation   ocean tides
Flames on Mars   and the alloy debris of spacecraft
Floating in the outer space
(They are lighter than a feather)

Massive Boulders Rolling in the Depths of the Yellow River

Just in a wind a massive boulder jumped into the Yellow River
Like a giant bird   it was dangling on a bluff on the verge of fracture
Just like a black monster kidnapped by time
It lost control by weariness from ready gestures but failed flights
The sky's carefree blue above the bluff
And some unexpected, mysterious dire straits or awakening
Knocked it out of control

On a night with the lonely starry sky
The massive boulder jumped into the Yellow River
I was startled into tears in a nightmare at the age of five

Growing up slowly   I accompanied my ferryman father
Bouncing with the dull waves of a grand canyon all the time
When I grew up   and returned home after a sojourn in a strange land
At a higher place   I thrust some other massive boulders
Successively down a cliff

Like playing a game of fall   I witnessed them collide with each other
Produce loud bangs and giant sparkles
(Sparkles making the broad daylight shiver and feel uneasy)
Scramble to win in the race   boom
And fall straight towards the abyss

For many years   I travelled afar and roved in the wind
It was in my incessant unsettled wander that I gradually discerned
The scene of the massive boulder jumping into the river
The giant boulder on the rumbling waves seemed to be light
Like an enormous paper mallard
Like a massive bird having purposely retracted its wings
Just from a high place it drifted down
Gliding and wafting

The wind rotated me as if it were rolling a massive boulder

However it is the Yellow River that will gyrate me eventually
Many years later   when I am too old
To turn again an enormous boulder in person
I will return to the riverside just like a child
Spend all day and every day there like an old bird
And behold how the massive boulders roll in the depths of the Yellow River
To occasionally speed up the weak obscure heart palpitation

Eventually when the Yellow River is aged and its water level keeps decreasing
The massive boulders no longer rotatable by the flow
Will be exposed from the center of the river one after another
Like numerous solitary lonesome messengers
All the massive boulders not worn down by roaring waves in their entire life
I will hug them as if we were old buddies
To let each other's sharp edges and horns
Cut deeper   and deeper
Cut off the wing-like clouds floating in the shallow water
Cut off the relationship between the Dragon Gate and a few little fish [1]
Perplexed by the starry sky and tranquility
Like nixies, in the last small pond

Cut off the massive boulders' flights as sinister as a strange bird's in a gale
From the bygones
Until they cut right at the medial axis between life and death
And cut off all the redundant stuff having plagued life and death for a
        long time
That even doesn't spare the demarcation between life and death
As if they were superfluous carnosities and cysts

---

[1] Dragon Gate (龙门; pinyin: lóng mén) can also be translated as Dragon's Gate. There is a
Chinese proverb that says "The carp has leaped through the Dragon Gate." It's a translation of
a five-character expression, "鲤鱼跳龙门" (pinyin: lǐ yú tiào lóng mén), which was originally
used as a metaphor for a person's success in passing very difficult imperial examinations,
required for entry into imperial administrative service. This expression is still used today to
communicate that if a person works hard enough, success will be achieved eventually.

Stray at the Littoral National Seagull Park

The Littoral National Seagull Park
A specialized dominion designed for birds from and about to fly towards
        the ocean
To prevent them from dying tired due to their inability to land and rest in
        a timely manner
And also for them to reproduce, parent, grow and inhabit
As I overlooked the warning sign of no entry, sightseeing, fishing or hunting
I entered the park by mistake   completely and utterly unaware
And didn't hesitate to head towards the depths for no reason

First startled by me were some sensitive storm petrels and seagulls
That hedgehopped over swiftly   skimmed the inky blue of an artificial lake
And then flitted a green facet of an original low-rise urban
        architectural complex
In the high-tech zone on the coast
And the landscape trees confined by layers of wire mesh fences
In an area between the facet and the seagull park
Because of the birds' continuous collisions   and incessant flight back
        and forth
The flight of this flock of miscellaneous seafowl
Was hasty as if they were fleeing with little heed to orientation

Realizing being lost   I felt somewhat confused and embarrassed
In anxiety   while looking around
I beheld the meadow and garden fringing the seagull park
A group of gardeners with white mosquito head nets under the
        scorching sun
Were trimming a forest of avenue trees in a hewing manner
And shearing the floss-cloud-like exuberance and viridity of the meadow
While remaining indifferent to my series of shouts for help
Of the few serene boulevards laid out in front of me
Each seemed to be endless   as if they had all led to
An expanse of moorland imprisoned by the yonder
Or to some uncharted coastal territory with no exits

The national seagull park   its densely distributed forest belts
Predominantly almost wild and natural   without a transitional
            growth period
And its quiet and secluded trails with barely any trace of artifact
Are places which the flitting storm petrels and seagulls
Could easily gather in or abandon
As a disoriented intruder of this forbidden area
I must brace myself to keep going alone
To walk out alone

The Spring of River, Crow and Plastic Bag

The crows scrambling with cranes for nests
Are still living on bluffs
As if the North and its great plains with a deafening harsh voice
Were still inhabiting in its classical times
When the spring comes
They casually renovate their old nests
They are still fond of white clouds
And flying around as freely as the clouds
Just like the cranes

The river clarified by sand grains   sources from the clouds
Or the yonder mountains heaped up like clouds
Or even an old well brimmed with water
Layers of artemisias break through the trash on the riverbanks
Grow up gradually   and look like they have prevailed and thrived
Behind a vast expanse of verdantly lush wheat fields
In a sandstorm which has lasted for an entire week
And which can't even be reined or blocked by the Qin Mountains
Before the river reaches the extremity of the great plain
Its gingerly course stops in a timely manner

The water from the South-North Water Transfer Project is greenish for its
          own sake
Its nerves are too tense and tightened
As if it were a flying crane
A flying crow   and flying white and dark clouds
Posing as a white crow and a white cloud, a white plastic bag
Flies over the plain   as if it could travel farther than the discontinued river
It is flying together with a crow and a puff of white cloud

A Tree Blacklisted by a Felling Company

Every year a tree bears rich fruits at a high place beyond people's reach
And unreachable even by stones cast by people
That either are consumed by a few birds or fall by themselves

On the tree lives a family of birds resembling both phoenixes and
      crested ibises
Fragile yet beautiful   timid yet elegant
They nest in a deep dense shade more concealed than the big ripe fruits
Reproduce and parent   without making a scene   or dropping excrement
As if they wanted to spend their entire life in silence

The tree   is inhabiting in the depths of a narrow and small lane
With its massive root system stretching into the darkness of the strata instead
      of the sky for water
Some roots are so brawny   as to have inadvertently broken an underground
      water pipeline
Which has irritated the municipal management company multiple times
Also because it has never managed to control the wobbling of its giant curled
      boughs in a gale
It accidentally crashed the double-glazed soundproof glass of some
      neighboring high-rise dwellers
Which has caused some real big shot home-owners to feel sullen and sulky
Its trunk has been engraved with heaps of scars of hatred left by knife cuts
Its giant curled boughs that love to whisper incessantly with the welkin
      and moonlight
Have suffered plural hacks more merciless than the strike of a thunder

The tree has experienced the transition   from wilderness to a small town and
      a metropolis
It has lived for so long   as to have become a sprite
It has been a long time   since the barnacles of resentment started
      to accumulate
Recently the news says very clearly that
It has been formally listed by the municipal management company
On its upcoming blacklist of an urban felling project

Dark Tempest of Last Year

The dark tempest of last year
Definitely changed the directions of the few mountains familiar to us
And of a few rivers unfamiliar to us
A congress of black crows darker than the dark tempest
Also last year   changed the direction of the megacity where I lived
And of its firmament with which I just started to get familiar
And in which planes had forcibly occupied the flight routes of birds
The artificial rainmaker of a super hotel and his superb windshield wiper
Scraped off the black glass resembling the dark storm of the super skyscraper
And thereby altered the deep sleep of the dark storm in the depths of
        the skyscraper
Brought the super moon of this superb city   the black moon
To choose the place where the sun rises, to ascend with Apollo
And forced a dole of grey doves perching at the airport
And a group of outlanders lost in the strange land like the grey doves
To divert, in the dark storm
The color and direction of their return home

Observer of the Egg of the World

Like a bird lingering at an empty nest
He alone is remaining by the side of an uninhabited empty mountain
With only ferocious beasts, clouds and mists

Over time, the man having tamed himself by emptiness in the
      empty mountain
Having gradually mastered the skills to manage the jungle and
      rock crevices
And appreciating the boiling hot heartbeat in the twinkling of starlight
Can even in the tenebrosity, as clearly as in broad daylight
Discern a dinosaur and a bull colliding with each other
And competing to pass through
In a pinhole of the world as fine as a spider silk

The world is so immense   that nothing is too strange
He has even observed an unprecedented enormous egg
The egg of the world that can only be hatched
By the endless emptiness of the universe

Today Your Soul Should Choose to Sail in the Ocean
—— Worshiping Qu Yuan, Minister of Three Imperial Clans,
on Tomb-Sweeping Day in 2016

Exerting willpower and stamina as powerful as a captive devil
The man has used his three thousand *zhang* of long hair to confront
            the river [1]
And to confront the three thousand years of time
Today three thousand dragon boats disperse the fish and clear the way
            for you
Today should be the day when you depart for the ocean to attend
            your appointment
Your route should be the route of a big fish
And the route of time and revenants that, in the center of ten thousand
            fish eggs
Flood towards ten thousand oceans
As if they were resurrected from death

Today the great long river rolls on endlessly
Just like thousands of branches pointing at the sky at the same time
And thousands of rivers all heading towards the ocean
Those fish that have eaten so many birth control pills and become chubby
            and narrow-minded
Those fish that, in the toxins discharged endlessly by secret channels
Are sometimes sober, and at other times, unconscious
Today you must allow them to shoot the rapids with you together
To voyage towards the direction that will lead you all to the ocean

Today you take with you the wind
The majesty of the cliffs on the riverbanks as well as the grey fog
And also the patience of the rivers and their pain for losing water
Today's ocean is as grand and lonely as before
Whale-like isles and islets come clearly into view
Shoals of fish formed by your soul as well as those of many others
Today will all start the voyage on the vast ocean
Wish you smooth sailing and bon voyage

[1] *Zhang* (丈; pinyin: zhàng) is a unit of length standardized as $3^1/_3$ meters in 1984 in mainland China.

Gripping Stars at a Maritime Museum

A star is a grain of sand on the seashore
That comes from an unfortunate clam
Unfortunately pushed up to the sand beach by an ocean tide
That can never again return to the bowels of the ocean
A pair of unlucky seashells
Inadvertently broken by a sea jackal feeling faint from hunger
It cannot retain a priceless pearl worth several cities
But a grain of sand
However when it is deceased
Followed by the demise of the entire ocean
The grain of sand is spilled out from the broken shucks
As if a star were sifted out from the aquamarine blue of the firmament
After time or the universe is crushed

At this moment   at the maritime museum on the coast
I am gripping a fistful of sand
Just like grasping a cluster of stars
Whose body temperatures can no longer be found

Oral Narrative of an Ocean Nurturer

After drifting on the ocean for a few days
What can I wash clean in salt
As a man fond of being empty handed
And captivated by the coolness of an ocean breeze
Who hauls up buckets, one after another, of the inky blue of the ocean
And then splashes it towards the sky again and again
Where can I take the bucket to
As a man loving to draw water with a bamboo basket
Enjoying exploitation of a flying bird for navigation
And having fished out onto the deck
A tilted dilapidated beacon and its iron scraps
I can only come back with a starry sky and sadness
I can only be a man tortured by shame and abashment
Under the cover of the darkness   the quietude of the night
I can only return ashore barefooted
With the drowsy bird from the mast

After drifting on the ocean for a few days
In a bare-handed   good-for-nothing voyage
I have only brought back a seafowl
A big and dull   useless bird
A monstrous bird
I will nurture it
As if I were rearing a pet
As if I were fostering an ocean
At the depths of the continent only reachable by a somnambulist
In the manner of tending a dream or a flowery cloud
I will nurture it

The Qin Mountains

When the entire world becomes a heap of shaggy ruins
The Qin Mountains remain   they
Are still full of faith   just like a fluffy deity
Waiting at ease, gracefully and comfortably
For the birth of the next mankind
By unbridled accumulation of its grass, trees
Broken stems and deeply secluded valleys

When the Qin Mountains become a heap of shaggy ruins
A deity still remains on the meadow at their pinnacle
When the deity creates the next world
He will surely follow the example of the Qin Mountains
And emulate the way the Qin Mountains grow grass and nurture trees
And the way they produce elves and transform monsters
So as to let the world, in a natural and spontaneous manner
Sprout up from the ruins

Moorland Is My Friend

The man with a very big forehead gleaming with light
Far and deep-sighted   with the light of objects
Directly contained in the depths of his vision
Has come down from the highland at the end of the moors
From some yonder place more recondite than the moorland
I've only met him occasionally on the street
As soon as I see his broad bright countenance
Looking like that he can hold many moorlands in his heart
I flip palpating with excitement   engrave him in my mind
Ever since then I have too become obsessed with
Interacting with the wilderness
Now with the lapse of time
The moorland has become a friend of mine
Even those wild flowery clouds having scurried in the moors
For so long as to have strayed inadvertently
Have become my friends
A fluttering black butterfly   dumped by its girlfriend
Its gigantic beauty and frustration
As well as its solo flight colliding with the entire moorland
Are also my friends

I have been deeply infatuated with the moors
My shadow and I
Including those I have come across only once and then will never forget
Who once showed up in the moorland and then disappeared from there
They and their shadows
Are all kept in my mind like the relatives I keep thinking about
We are all part of the moorland

Nest of the Tenebrosity

Actually many birds are very impatient of brooding in a nest
After the nestlings are hatched they will henceforth never return
In fact many birds don't really have a nest
Woods are their homes
Branches are their homes
Woods and their shades
Are their homes

Many birds   such as crows
Always come in the murk
Just like a compact cluster of smithereens darker than the darkness of
        the dark
The tenebrosity activates them so exceptionally
That they fly in the center of the dark
Without descending for a long, long time
Their silent flights shaking the darkness
Are their homes

Kua Fu Chasing Clay Balls in the Park

A little five-year-old boy was shaping clay balls in a glade of the park
He molded one clay ball   five clay balls   seven clay balls
That were all made of clay wetted by his own urine
Then he started to chase just like a dung beetle chasing a ball of dung
The clay spheres created by himself
He chased them so hard that they rolled around and around aimlessly
So hard that he himself rolled all over the ground
Until they rolled out of the great lawn of the park
And arrived at the lakeside in the park
Without any hesitation
He then chased them until they all fell into the water

When he pushed too hard   lost his equilibrium
Fell into the water following hard on the heels of the clay balls
His father yelled: Kua Fu! Kua Fu! [1]
Dashed over like a ferocious tiger
And plunged into the water

[1] Kua Fu (夸父; pinyin: kuā fù) is a giant in Chinese mythology who wished to capture the sun.

II

Dangerous Nests
of the Dream Clinic

Holding My Tongue at the Subway All Day Long

To escape or adjust my relationship with a city
I prefer to go to the subway and hold my tongue
I wandered through the subway the whole day
Wearing strong dark sunglasses   pretending to be a loafer
Naturally keeping an almost refusing attitude towards
And distancing with everything just a few feet away
Including those occasionally accosting me for directions or a chat
This guaranteed my free exercise of sensitivity and idiosyncrasies
In observation of obscure and mysterious things

A piece of soil accidentally brought to the platform by an outlander from
        another city
The dust or alike amassed together furtively in a corner
A shoe crowded out by the wave of passengers jostling one another
An ungainly walking blind man having to be assisted by a kind-hearted guy
These were the things I was able to spot and so should others

When a train shuttled through the subterranean tunnel like a beetle
A spider and its cobweb were hanging under the vault
On the other side of the windows flashing by   imitating a caveman
Someone had painted the entire wall with prehistoric monsters
A melancholy guitarist had halted the performance while leaning against a
        wall alone
A dwarf duck waddled forward apparently in despise of the masses
A subway patrol in a special uniform   jostled against the crowd from place
        to place
Snooped tirelessly around all the corners for shadows   poker-faced
And look at others as if he had been driving nails
These were the things I was able to observe while others were unlikely able to

I strolled in the subway all day long
Maybe I was too lucky   all the people I met the whole day were from
        other cities
Eventually I didn't utter a single word for the whole day

And I spent the entire day in silence

The strength of the sunglasses   instilled in me, amongst the surging waves
        of people

The intimacy not only with the entire world   but also with myself

The intimacy seemingly felt through a sheet of glass

Not only real but more than real

Earth Is a Balloon With a Pain in Its Heart

Earth is light, wafting in the air like a balloon
As light as a balloon with a pulp other than a peel
As light as a puff of air
Lethal air, whether one puff more or one puff less

On Earth, the weight of elephants   of mountains   of massive boulders
Including the weight of the oceans in the bowels of the soaked seas
The weight of the whales swinging in the basket of the oceans
Including those accurately calculable   such as the weight of a needle
And the weight of the entire Earth   some people cherry-pick the light and
       shirk the heavy
And even regard a thread of silk as a load of thirty thousand catties [1]
Actually in terms of heaviness and lightness   their relationship
Is only a matter of a puff of air
And an art showing the outcome in merely three to five minutes
By a gas by the name of oxygen

A man is living in the mundane world
A bird is soaring in the vault of heaven
And an airplane is drifting either above or under the clouds
Whether or not you are a well-behaved discreet person
Whether or not you are a well-behaved discreet tree
Whether or not you are a well-behaved discreet bird
Whether or not you are an unmeasurable pain in Earth's heart
Maybe you don't know the answers yourself
But Earth does, sailing in the air like a balloon

Earth is a good planet floating like a balloon
Proficient in the art of lightness   the art of a puff of air
With a pain in its heart   and its stomach brimmed with bitterness
And the weight of the same amount of salt in the ocean that pickles
       the wounds
It even doesn't tell those people unable to discriminate between lightness
       and heaviness

It once experienced
The weight of the balloon with a pain in its heart
And the weight of Earth as light as that of the balloon
Only measurable by the balloon
Average people can't discern them
It doesn't speak out either

---

[1] The catty (斤; pinyin: jīn) is a traditional Chinese unit of mass used across East and Southeast Asia. In mainland China, the catty has been rounded to 500 grams and is referred to as the market catty. Thirty thousand catties equals to one thousand *jun* (钧; pinyin: jūn). Since the catty is more widely known than the *jun*, the source text with the meaning of "one thousand *jun*" (千钧; pinyin: qiān jūn) is replaced by "thirty thousand catties."

The World and Its Dangerous Nests

This is a place where gales rage tirelessly
Where vehement winds damage trees   so they can hardly grow
Where a tree can rarely bear any fruit when growing up
Where flights have a home whilst birds can barely find one
It has the smoothness and curvature of ocean waves
A man fond of the scenery of a desert
Roams without any purpose
And seems to be gradually approaching the extremity of the universe
The tree he has encountered sporadically is extremely lonely
Drenched in scars of wounds
That are the cut marks of axes and chisels left from an unknown era
The bird nests on the tree are especially over dense
Just like fruits lading all the branches
Just like fruits
Hiding in the hardly reachable deep shade
The only things that exist for a reason are the electricity pylons
That usher the power lines crossing over the moors all the way to the horizon
With a willpower more solitary than that of a tree   and some outrageousness
On the nearby high voltage power lines   some places
Are incredibly clustered with flocks of silent birds
The electricity pylon nearest to the flocks
Is just like an over-trimmed tree
On which many remarkably noticeable dangerous nests are aggregated
That seem to be living outside the world
But bear it with equanimity

Fish-Eating Man and Potato-Eating Man

The man growing up on the riverside in the South
By devouring black fish from white water
Rice eels from the yellow mud of a paddy field
And the eggs of wild swans from deep reed marshes
Loves to paint with watercolor pens   unique paintings
He has drawn a water ghost after the look of a giant salamander
Qu Yuan drowned in a river with his fluttering long beard
And a seven-spotted python, in moonlit reeds as dense as a forest
Coiling the enormous epic moon as if it were safekeeping
In its dreams an infant for someone

The man growing up in the northern moors and sandy areas
And eating potatoes barbecued in a bonfire
And plucked birds wrapped in clay and roasted in fire
Is a man fond of painting on the sands and rocks
Drawing the sun after a sunflower
Dark clouds after crows
Blossoms after stars
And the dens and lairs of aliens
After an unclaimed empty giant egg-shell

The southern fish-eating man and the northern potato-eating man
Are both masters of cruising and flying techniques
Exceptionally sensitive men
And experts able to directly observe
The secrets of the flights of UFOs

Writing Lyrics for a Rocker at a Subway Passage

This spring loves the seemingly rotten loneliness
The heavy snow resembles invertedly grown thorns in the sky
With six varieties of lascivious blades on their hexagonal vertices
Falling like sharp nails
In this remote desolate northern area
The man trekking in this strange land with a heavy backpack
Is like a piece of timber from an anonymous tree
Hewed and whittled many times   and carved unevenly
With his gloomy forehead
And brilliant facial expression

This trekker exhaling hot air from his mouth
With eyes as sharp as fireballs
Witnesses how a gale destroys a train
Blows away the tents and hitching posts in the wild
And chaps the faces of the pedestrians
The gale has whirled away and scattered loosely
A green train and its shattered glass on a strange land
They obstruct the road with dead-looking half-open ghost eyes
The road you are going to pass

In this blustery spring   with a susurrating snow squall
The damp and rotten loneliness   like the snow in the shadow
Is growing furtively like cockroaches

Letters to the Clouds

Compose a letter every day
Which has nothing to do with love
Nor lonesomeness
Nor transmission of information
Nor the falling of tree leaves
Skimming across the window
Towards the dark
Like anonymous plumes

Write a letter every day
With a pen dipped in the moorland zephyr
And a fine dust inadvertently sodden by a raindrop
Under the starry sky

Write to Beijing   write to New York
Write to the London subway clock forgetting to tell time
Write to the man facing a cliff alone and painting on rocks
On an anonymous island in the depths of the Pacific Ocean

Write to the wild child
Who wears red in all seasons
Crisscrosses the railway station every day carrying luggage
Grows up by drinking blue seawater
And is taken ashore from the ocean by a navigator

Write to the little girl in the neighborhood
Who is like a heister or a hooker
Vanishing into the blue day in day out
Nowhere to be seen nor remembered by her name

Write to the clouds
To the kites hanging slantingly on the treetops and cloud acmes
That frequently wake me up from my middle-aged reveries
And that weep due to their decadent and defeated suspension

Grey Overcast Sky Above the Bell Tower

Evening clouds hanging low above the Bell Tower   swallows
In the sky bound by bandage-like lights
Dart up and down like arrows   sail like water dabblers
As if they were testing the dim light of night
Like grey khaki fabric and as melancholy and indolent as a cat
With gloomy clouds draping and dripping with water

Evening clouds hanging low   gulps of swallows soaring together
Curling up like a cat on the cement floor
Behind a marble column of the Bell Tower
I am a sleeper muffled in a plastic sheet
And a man having dreamt of a rainfall
And attempted to produce chimes by striking a bell
Soaked in the rain like a mushroom

I have also dreamt of a bellman holding a grayish blue glass cat
After the attack by the dark clouds and swallows   unable to tear
        himself away
He pillowed a large cluster of shattered pieces from the grayish blue glass cat
And slept dispiritedly and aggrievedly like a castoff
In the raindrops all over the streets

A Man's Knife Glint, Moonlight and Starshine

This is a man with a shadow and height only measurable by a tall wall
And a plain yet dangerous mind higher than tree canopies and clouds
And hanging in the sky crossed by kites and planes
Someone saw him in the woods under the moonlight
Practicing alone a body-shrinking technique like catching fish in a tree
As a member of the municipal rescue squad
With the talent of clambering up an edifice and breaking its skylight
      like a spider
He cuts glass as precisely and efficiently as incising the skin
Once he washed absolutely clean some people of a sudden death in glass
And displayed them on the other shore no one can reach
No one can closely observe his
Countenance more blurred than starlight
And his silhouette sporadically showing up on the unreachable other shore
With some dispiritedness freed by him as well as some frustration

This is a man who circumvents the sidewalks and narrow lanes
To saunter alone in the moorland
And tirelessly sweeps with wild grass and branches
The knife glints unleashed by his gloomy countenance
That look like the shines faded out ever after someone gets knifed to death

He will rehabilitate himself into another person
One who can return to the life on this shore
While being unnoticeable to anyone

Three Poets or the Most Melancholy One

The saddest and most melancholy poet   is in the South
With rare birds unaccustomed to high flight
A farmer whose paddy field is destroyed by excessive rainfalls
Isn't fond of looking into afar   except nagging
However if it happens to an indignant poet it will be different
He would probably be somewhat like Qu Yuan   in a vast white mist
When no one else could see anything
He would see the whiteness of the river
Blanched by a blowing autumn gale
As white as a morning dew or as pale as a lifeless person
And the pallidness, like that of land or a dead fish
That surfaces and submerges alternately in the heavy darkness
Of the river that seems to be gradually darkening and sinking
After peach blossoms and roseate clouds are blown down by a gale

The saddest and most melancholy poet   is in the North
Under the Big Dipper and some smaller stars
In a vast white mist   when no one else can see anything
He witnesses electric-arc-like fireflies (twinkling stars in the sky
Gleaming fireflies on the ground) and the wet glistens
Ploughed out by earthworms from the bowels of the earth
As well as the dimness of the land and its sparkling stars

The saddest poet   in a city swamped with outlanders from afar
Is like a wooden post with the temperament of a shadow
With somewhat unknown origin   sometimes laid aside on a square
Sometimes hiding away (for a few successive years)
Sometimes blowing in suddenly from the vast white mist
So indiscernible as to be like the shadow of something
And yet so unrejectable

With a violent tendency out of boredom and destitution   homeless
After heaping up a pile of stones at a corner of the street
He tosses a stone
Just to hit another one

An Aesthete's Nails and Hammer

Grabbing a fistful of nails in one hand
And a hammer in the other, the man
Is busy finding cracks all over the world every day
Places in which he could hammer a nail
He is looking for cracks on walls
Cracks on eggs
Cracks on bluffs
Sometimes when exhausted and meditating
He even imagines alone in his mind
The cracks on Mars and anonymous stars
Having ever been tortured badly by failures and mishaps
The aesthete harsh in his intention and endeavors
Chooses to make a living by driving nails
He is fond of long and strong nails
And has acquired the most suitable hammer for himself
Now every day he is fussy about picking and choosing
Every day looking for the type of nearly perfect cracks
Those as delicate as the tree holes made by a woodpecker
Those that can rotate the universe and stars furtively
Those that can only be snooped and mastered by God
Rhythmically subtle cracks
He will swing his hammer
In the most accurate and ruthless manner
Directly punch a nail
In the juncture as vital as the heart of the world
A place no one can disassemble

A Man With a Horrible Dent in His Head

Head down he plays with a knife all the time
With the knife he pares apples   peels pineapples
The dent in his head
Is as big and deep as a bowl
Big and deep enough to hold
One mine
Two fists
Big and deep enough for a hen to dwell in
Lay eggs or hatch chickens
In the plastic-rimmed paper box next to him
Are some coins and small bills from passengers
Thin on the ground   countable at one glance
Under the umbrage of trees at a street corner
The man is soliciting mercy for himself
Refusing no comer   stopping no leaver
He is paring apples and pineapples   without lifting his head
Giving it to everyone to enjoy after they drop him a coin
A man with a horrible dent in his head

Someone has directly dropped a coin in the dent in his head
Neither humble nor arrogant   with neither hatred nor anger
Just like playing a game   he shakes his head tirelessly
To let the coin swirl continuously in the dent
Giving up any sense of humiliation   he bows in thanks
While engrossing himself in paring apples   peeling pineapples
Waiting for those willing to enjoy them

Cliff With Cranes

Smog and enthusiastic tourists have been subverting
The cliff with herded cranes
And the verdant lushness of pines and cypresses on the cliff
As well as the gurgling white waterfalls
Hanging down like curtains from a high place
When the dripping wet bluff
(Seemingly with the power to deliver the universe) is subverted
Even when the smog is subverted as well   the running water
Sinks into the bowels of the mountains like a secret
Exhuming the valley and the riverbed with piled-up insensate stones
And also plastic bags   instant noodle bowls   beer bottles
And filthy and greasy domestic waste with complex ingredients

I behold a quiet lonesome scavenger
Like a woodman returning to his old profession in the mountains with his
        legacy skills
Like a failed angler
Or like a bear having lost its territory
In the depths of the deeply secluded lonely valley
With a plastic sunhat on his head   heavy trash on his back
Sometimes searching and forging ahead in the wasteland on the riverbed
Sometimes clambering up the cliff bare-handed

Falling White Snow and Blooming Red Plum Blossoms

Lonesome snow is racing on the lonely dark clouds
Racing in the North   on the northern dark clouds
On its way to the ocean
Southing direct unobstructedly   racing in the South

Dark clouds are speeding, and white snowflakes falling profusely
In both the South and the North
In the entire world
The whiteness of the boundless white snow
I know the Pacific Ocean needs it   you need it
An eagle and an accipitral steel aircraft too need it
A kind of emphasized downward temperature calculator
A kind of whiteness about mutually crucial things like lips and teeth
The whiteness of the white snow drifting profusely
The dark clouds need it
The world and its furry-fuzzy disordered whiteness need it
The redness of red lips with white teeth needs it

Falling white snow   blooming red plum blossoms

I know at a place with no snow
Blooming red plum trees are silent
So are the blooming white plum trees

The dark clouds are dashing   white snowflakes are falling
Falling above the ocean
And in the world's sleeping depths at its end
Falling white snow   blooming red plum blossoms
White plum blossoms as fluffy as white snowflakes
Are blooming as well

Aborted Visit to the Yellow River in the Central Plains

Getting off the train   alighting from a plane
Coming down from the mountains with lone residents
Passing through many places like a spinning gyroscope
Going east out of the Central Shaanxi Plain
By passing through the Tong Pass   and entering Zhengzhou City
I always wanted to have a look, at a place closest to
The Yellow River, at how it traversed the Central Plains

I was always afraid that the legendary inevitable river
If I visited it a few years later
Would become a river of occasionality

Ascending from the bottom of the plains, Zhengzhou's suburbs
The car and yellow dust
On the same road and towards the same direction
Meandered like a beaten rundown dragon
With some kind of ennui and helplessness hidden in its anger

A little before noon   on a dead end road
The car almost unexpectedly tumbled into a loess abyss
And thereby aborted my journey to see the Yellow River
From a car window   the clay Central Plains
At its roadside stood an agrestic rustic beheaded tree
Seemingly made of clay too

I always wanted to take a closer look at the Yellow River
But the plan came to an end at a place nearest
To the tree decapitated for an unknown reason, before my eyes
As if it were a tree of destiny
And also a tree of occasionality

A Narrow Escape From a Breathtaking Encounter at an Ancient Ferry on the Yellow River

The ferryman on the Yellow River fell asleep on the other shore
So soundly   that several batches of people couldn't rouse him by whoops
As a ranger anxious to head westwards   to an unknown destination
Who had spent most of his life taking delight in collecting winds and clouds [1]
And who had seen enough in his life   and thereby was inured to the unusual
I had to take time to wait at the ferry on this shore with patience
Until the curtains of night fell
Until another bunch of people came to wait for the ferry boat at dusk
And had a close run-in with me in the corvine darkness

I later heard that it was a gang dealing in historical relics and robbing tombs
Digging not only others' ancestral tombs   but also their own
And living a life by sacking the heads of the dead and their own
In shabby gunny bags
I was so sensitive   as to have perceived in a timely manner that
Some kind of ominous atmosphere emerged suddenly after their arrival
More impatient than I   more eager to cross the river
They couldn't wait   but started immediately to aggregate around me
With a hostile and suspicious look brimmed with murderous intention
Pretending to ask me for a lighter they drew near to me a few times
And took turns eyeing and testing me   among them two guys
Wielded a Luoyang shovel as if brandishing a deadly weapon [2]
And hewed sparkles on a rock   while giving out menacing words:
When crossing the river later on they would chop off the ferryman's head
As if cutting a gourd into a ladle and then throw it into the Yellow River
I knew they were testing by disguising their true intention
My suspicious origin   if I were an undercover rushing to be
Ahead of them but interrupted on my journey by the river
A warning that I shouldn't take the risk of impeding them

"The river flushes nonstop toward the twilight like galloping horses
The ferryman is sinking into a deep sleep like a dead crow"
I took out my notebook   postured as a scholar

Stayed away at a corner alone and loudly read my newly written poem
And purposely distanced me from them with an aloof indifferent manner
As if they hadn't existed at all
As if I hadn't cared about them at all
As a poet deeply shocked by the waves on the disorderly stony shoal
With a chest seriously stabbed by the Yellow River at dusk
Having the silence and rugged tendency of an abandoned rock
I exploited the simplest method
To conceal my true colors
And the true colors of a group of grave-robbers armed with
        murdering swords [3]
And thereby escaped the jaws of danger

I heard at dusk as dead as a crow
Their laughter and chatter as lively as a crow's

[1] "Collecting winds" is a literal translation of "Cai Feng" (采风; pinyin: cǎi fēng), which is normally translated as "field trips," "collecting folk songs," or "understanding popular customs." In China, Cai Feng is a popular activity for artists to collect raw materials and seek inspiration in places well-known or special.

[2] The Luoyang shovel (洛阳铲; pinyin: luò yáng chǎn) is one of the most important tools in Chinese archeology. It was originally invented by grave-robbers in the Luoyang City, the central city in ancient Central Plains.

[3] "Murdering swords" is a short translation for "Gui Tou Dao" (鬼头刀; pinyin: guǐ tóu dāo), a sword for beheading persons sentenced to death in ancient China.

Spring Rain and Mist of the Central Plains

Rain and mist drops are splattering April's wheat fields
And a wide and quiet river
In the season to hew weeds that hasn't arrived in time
A postmenopausal woman obliged to stay at home in the village
Under a maple tree in the afternoon
Is flagrantly altering an aqueduct from an old era
At the night of toil   the water rejects the moon
Due to its murkiness under the moonlight
None of these can hold any longer her bad mood and narrow-mindedness
Articles broken by her are so many as to overload a truck
A large expanse of wheatland she has trampled
Under the cover of the rain and mist
Seems not to be able to stand bolt upright again

This spring of the Central Plains is not very smooth
The quiet wide river has forborne itself again and again
A caterwauling cat   and another cat
Have left each other without a goodbye before finishing mating
Rainfall from dark clouds has darkened a scarecrow's black hat
And also the bird nest
On the poplars lining one edge of the wheat field
That has hidden in the spinney since the Republic of China
As well as an old steamer, with a black iron canopy
In the wide quiet river, that can only be spotted
At a place as high as the bird nest

The spring in the raindrops is continuing rotting away
So are a field of bursting watermelons with excessive watery pulps in the mist
The person hidden in an empty-nest-like village afraid of travelling afar
Nowadays is also a person hidden on the river most time
And a person having lost his direction
With the only ferryboat starting to leak
Overdrinking unhappily   he sometimes throws liquor bottles to strike
         the river

Sometimes runs to a hiding place in the tussocks on the riverbank
      like a ghost
Just as a wild mallard on the verge of laying an egg

In the Central Plains' spring   a drunkard squatting in the grass but laying
      no egg
In his slumber far and rotting like a tattered batting
Is dreaming of a train wriggling and squirming slowly like a snake
And also like a wild beast under the moonlight

On the boat of the big river in the raindrops and thick fog
Illuminated is a lamp with the light seeming not only falling but also rotting

Going Northwards, at the Height of a Bird

You can also be at the height of a bird
In another way heading northwards, northwards

At an altitude above ten thousand meters
Where only a compass has directions   whilst the world
Has none
The aircraft is wobbling its steel skeleton
The oxygen becoming thinner and thinner is wobbling your skeleton
From one point to another
The clumsy flight is doomed to have
A rough time caused by the fog
Merging into one with the sky inside the sky   in its vastness
At a higher place   in the sky beyond the sky
Clouds are waiting for you to chase without batting an eye
So is the emptiness

Going northwards   at the height of a bird
Like sun-chasing Kua Fu   the place where a bird will land
Is also the place you will touch down
If you descend too heavily   over rapidly
Like a super heavy bomb unexplodable by a falling bomb
You should be glad to accept
The consequences of chasing northwards

Black and White in the Bright Blue Sky

On the plain blows a pregnant wind
The bright blue of the firmament
The grass seeds accidentally scattered in the wilderness last year
And the cherry blossoms so dreadfully pale like deep snow
As to enable the city and its spring
To be more like a fictional snow
All send chills down my spine

The blow of a wind in late spring has opened
The vast bright blue tinted with some kind of blur above the plain
And carried away a helicopter as white as snow that has mistakenly entered it
Its directionless hum is like the weep of a little underground ghost
Shortly after take-off it becomes as dark as a black bird
And thereby sends chills down my spine

Early summer's zephyr brings the scents of lemon and cheap perfume
Those young married women in skirts as ghostly white as snow
Are inopportunely having their photos taken together with trees
Which coincides with the scene in the urban park
In which a fictional white swan has wound up in the weeds since last spring
And an old windmill has dilapidated into a heap of obsolete materials

It brings a real white swan having lost its footing and thereby attempting
To approach the pinnacle of the Bell Tower   to feel a shiver down its spine

Blank and Melancholy

I have always been searching for a blank stretch of land
(Even if it's only a scene of bleakness and desolation)
Or an expanse of moorland
(Even if it's drenched in strange clouds and fogs)

That is the absolutely empty land I experience repeatedly in dreams
The land without the background of rivers or mountains
Or the background of the firmament   or of a city
Or a historical, family name, or gender-based background

That is the self-indulged journey
Of an outlander straying in a place away from home
Obsessed with some kind of inhuman bewilderedness
Seeking relief but hopelessly
Attempting to abandon his soma as well
And trying to exclude all the protagonists
As well as the heights of all the birds and planes

As an overlooker   always at another place
A place whence I can overlook both self and other overlookers
I am familiar with the route to the blank land in dreams
And also understand thoroughly the ways of escape

The method of finding a way out is:
I have witnessed in person the fall of stars   so light
That it, like a drizzle of past and time
Has filled all the tangible blanks with intangible darkness
But has disappeared without a trace like a dreamland and soul
Landing any capture in vain

Blue Boy Smuggling Birds' Nests up the Trees

The blue kid   has a body as crystally bluish as the ocean

The ocean's dark blue lit by a beacon
Grayish blue completely invaded by sunshine and thick fogs
Blue belly gashed by giant plowing ships
And dark chest effervescing big bubbles and then filled up
Again and again by the horizon and sorrowful stars
Are all the blue of the blue kid
As staunch and steadfast as sea rocks
As capricious and vagarious as the ocean
And hardly controllable by a base person or devil

Afar in the ocean   quietly enduring the pain of the mundane world
The blue kid alone is furtively transporting nests on trees
Such curious and dangerous work   piles of endangered eggs
He must be as cool as a cucumber like a senior carrier
And remain daring and scrupulous in venturing his life
Those nests   he will mount among the stars
Place on the moon and its fragrant tea olive [1]
And put inside the universe with nebulas gliding like bird flocks

The blue kid secretly transporting nests towards the stars
The planner and designer of the trees of stars
Wants birds, planes and spacecraft
To take off at the blue lake where he dives while holding his breath

He wants doves, birds and even blue peacocks with their showy clumsiness
To fly hither and thither in flocks and musters
In the thick dense shade of the trees of stars
In and out the superficially changed nests he has stealthily transported to there

[1] In traditional Chinese folklore, it says that there is a cinnamon tree on the moon. Since last imperial China, many scholars have mistaken the cinnamon tree as Osmanthus fragrans, sweet olive, or fragrant tea olive. Some contemporary scholars translate the tree as "the katsura tree."

Dream Clinic in a Mirror

In the mirror stands a maiden possessed by a devil
With long hair cascading down freely like a black gauze

The maiden   with red teeth and white lips
In the unclean April   the April days
Able to sniff the strong reek of a piece of glass
Eager to cause disturbances inside the body of a tiger
And hence appearing incomparably coquettish
A maiden forced to run to a bluff by a flood in her dream
And inquiring about her whereabouts on the breakfast table
In the entire April   suspects herself as an eggshell
Inside which a giant bird is giggling disheveled hard feathers
Neither dying   nor flying
But growing bigger and bigger   with a horriblish look

The maiden can't help getting coquettish in the entire April
The look of disheveled tresses is only posed for the mirror
How can she utter a word about her inexplicable tortured thoughts
When she recalls once again   in a nightmare and trance
A deceased person in the water with a face covered in hair called her name
She can't help perspiring profusely in the depths of the mirror
The mirror is dripping with sweat in the shadow of her body
Whilst the vase with artificial poppy flowers
On the dressing table behind her
Gives a terrifying scream and then falls into pieces

The seductive maiden observing self in the mirror in the entire April
With languish concealed in coquettishness like fire wrapped in paper
Chased by her own naked body in dreams
In the mirror of April   in a ginger and even furtive manner
Is fiddling with a rusty grenade
Damp strange-shaped gunpowder
Dazzling lipsticks   all kinds of unknown pigments
But still unable to obtain a protective amulet   to stop herself
From plummeting deeper and deeper in the nightmare

In the dream   her hair billows boundlessly like the ocean
Her body inflates endlessly like a colossus
And a balloon filled with water expanding bigger and bigger
That can't be any heavier or any lighter
That can't fly or find a way to fall
Just like a wasp hive with sleeping wasps inside
Hanging in the rain

Oh, April! In April
When she can neither sleep nor awake inside the jail of the mirror
And flowerpots accidentally break into pieces scattered on the ground
With no one to tidy up
The tiger in the maiden's dream pounces on her
And then the tigerish maiden wakes up
In her mirror as elusive as seawater

Nobody Can See the Shattering of an Angelic Lady's Heart

Like a top-heavy sunflower
The angelic lady gallops alone aimlessly in a spring zephyr
Seemingly with vertigo
No one can see her broken heart
But she can see   the remarkably increased bird nests in the trees
And the slowly hazing moors and their wretched weeds
Impeding the flights of butterflies and swallows

Galloping alone   on her own
The angelic lady has arrived at the bowels of the land
The unbridled spring breeze sobers her up
She trips over her light red skirt and falls heavily
After weeping for a while alone   with eyes brightened by tears
She sees a dragon fly, a fruit lover
Throwing the leftover kernel off the horizon like litter
An eagle chasing a skylark proficient in slimming techniques
A helicopter unfortunately colliding with a fish-shaped kite
And their fragments flying like fluttering petals in the rain
And eventually stacking together heavily

The spring land is endlessly empty and spacious
The spring moorland is full of luxuriant weeds
The spring sky is so azure blue
The spring angelic lady runs faster and farther than a wind
Nobody can see all that she can see
Nobody can see her shattered heart

By the Ocean

As always   like an unfortunate man
I see the bleak and desolate sea again   by the ocean
At the place where the sea and its dissolute froths rout
Mountain peaks and cliffs spiral up like pythons
And ascend into the blue of the sky   into the clouds
Into the gloomy dimness of the starry sky

Luckily however
By the ocean   atop a jagged, rugged cliff
I see again the bird that shouldn't be belittled or glanced
A plump clumsy bird
With disheveled feathers   quivering like a hedgehog
In temporary slumber on a tough boulder

It's brewing a thrilling and groundless flight
That can freely traverse dark clouds and a tornado
Like the fall of a star

Between Ocean and Revolution

The ocean is chasing northwards   upwards
The ascending lofty mountains
Craggy boulders   and the Revolutionary Museum
Reachable only by crossing the deep woods

Between the ocean and the revolution
A man respecting the revolution more than the ocean
Ushers us across a valley as undulant as the ocean
Many hills   and many mounds as abrupt as bluffs
Treasured in the museum for uprisers having jumped into the ocean
Are many old artifacts   old guns
Old cannonballs   old pictures   old angle bars
Involved in hand-to-hand combats
And old clothes drenched in the blood of martyrs
Including the decayed look of the old world
Mopped up by the ocean of the revolution
It hides behind the alps affording panoramic views of the ocean
In the deep dense shade of a valley mantled by soughing pines

Between the ocean and the revolution
All the mountains that rise by the ocean
Are more vigorous and flourishing than the ocean
All the directions originate from the ocean
We walk all the way down there   with warm limbs
The ocean starts to surge in our hearts

Three Maidens and Belated-Blooming Northern Cherry Blossoms

Low gloomy clouds   lowered the sky above the northern cherry
       blossom boulevard
The temperature   and also the belated cherry blossoms in the cold
Three maidens hugged cherry trees while shaking down raindrops
A wind lifted up their skirts as colorfully variegated as butterflies
And their voice as shrill piercing as variegated butterflies'

Low gloomy clouds   three northern maidens under the dark grey clouds
Twittered with their thrilled voices like colorfully variegated butterflies
Lifted up their colorful skirts in grass   tiptoed with ankles as thin as a bird's
And guts which, smaller than those of a bird, couldn't suppress screaming

The three maidens under the dark grey clouds
Fruitlessly seeking blooms on the northern cherry blossom boulevard
And shaking down raindrops from the trees again and again
In the bleak desolate yet somewhat mysterious wind over the park
Constantly pressed down their skirts as restless as butterflies
They didn't even know themselves   at that moment they looked like
Cherry blossoms blooming in the low temperature

Just like the anthesis disclosed inadvertently
While sleeping on the heart of the dark clouds
With a gloomy countenance slightly tinted by the dark clouds
And the coquettishness of a variegated butterfly
And implied by the colorful skirts spreading out
A little tiny provocative anthesis

Spring and Fairness

It was in spring   while enjoying the green at the moorland edge
While this girl was stretching out her neck and body
And inhaling the fragrance of flowers
On a tree or in the grass as exuberant as bushes
When I noticed the fairness of her neck and nape
The fairness of her arms
And the fairness that extended like lightning in secrecy
Along her almost naked chest and the wrinkles of her cleavage

My breath seemed to be hit by lightning
By fading vertigo and lethal lightness
And by falling and fragmentation

After exerting substantial effort to calm myself down
I saw the look in her eyes
The resilience of both spring water and a deep abyss
I couldn't refrain from imagining
If her hair had been kept a little longer   a little less delicate
She would have had the recklessness and restrained grace of waterfalls
Which would make her fairness more enchanting
And render the fairness of a scallion stalk, of a lotus root, and of a
            lotus flower
The fairness of the bright and shinning light
Glistened brilliantly by a fish jumping out of a pool
And the fairness as exquisite and moistening as a white gem
All suitable for her succinct and lively praise
A kind of praise rich in silky elasticity

However what was most suitable for her praise
Was still, in a fatal glance resembling lightning
The fairness sharper than a razor and more lethal than lightning
The delightful fairness that would even kill a crowd of people

Fluttering Leaves in Lonesome Northern Winter

Leaves are fluttering in lonesome northern winter
Many trees are towering on the other side of the enclosing wall
A skyscraping suburban hotel and the bell tower
Installed on its top floor like a symbolic decoration
Stand erect near the starry sky, dodging the fluttering leaves
And therefore seem to be far and solitary

In the lonesome northern winter there are few passengers
On a dark late night there are even fewer passengers
Except for the lone man sweeping the streets clean
And continuously sweeping the fallen leaves under the street lamps
In the umbrage of trees   the umbra of walls
And the shadow of the Bell Tower with a complicated background
The street-sweeper and his slowly moving silhouette
Are sometimes scraggy and elongated   other times a little bulky
While quivering like phantoms that can breathe
And frequently crisscrossing the darkness in a clumsy and sluggish way

Leaves are fluttering in lonesome northern winter
In the vast starry sky   remote and dim
Behind the stars are tinier stars
Abandoned in the azure sky like shards of glass
Whilst all these things on the land   like a large pile of baggage
Accidentally discarded by an outlander in a dream
Are showered by chilly and lonesome light and shade
Blurred and fuzzy
With some kind of grievance and abruptness resembling falling leaves

City and Its Underground Worker

Serving as an underground worker just like a gopher
I engage in the everyday work of crossing tunnels under the ground
Or digging out burrows deeper than before
Every day I clean the sludge, sewage, gravels and mixed garbage
Stuck in the underground passages as if clearing bowel obstruction
Wearing a headlamp continuously lighting up the path
On which I must venture forward or retreat when chased by death
Every day I experience the earth, the city and the darkness in its depths
The subterranean tunnels' wide openness resembling a giant's throat
Is like another world and its secrets
Like a bird loving to fly alone I keep watching
The secrets not only so myriad but also monotonous
Never put on the table
And only enjoyable by a gopher

The endless yet fatuous quietude of the tunnels
And the underworld's cast iron pipe networks as outrageously tortuous
        as roots
Require somnambulant willpower to contest with
Just like a gopher
I have been used to all of it
This sweet and eventful darkness

Scene at Dusk

A man having just gotten familiar with me on the train
And walked with me all the way from the train station
While chattering nonstop   at a T-junction of the city
With one way connecting to the ocean and twilight
And another connecting to the city hall square
Stopped abruptly
And lapsed into silence
As if I hadn't existed

Though I was more familiar with this city than a map
I was attracted to this garrulous talker
Seeming to be delivering a speech or self-talking
Not until then
Did I find out that I had stepped onto the wrong path
Up till then
I still couldn't discern whether or not he was from another city
Nor could I find out if he was hesitating or waiting at that moment
He had a kind of vacant contemptuous
Naturalistic countenance

The insensitive man
Didn't know I was secretly sizing him up
Taking him by surprise
I turned around and into a tunnel towards the ocean

The Man Cutting Down Trees

A tree is a bucket of clean bright shining spring water
A spotless, crystal clear water well
And a super penetralium in which
The earth, ocean and wide blue yonder
Exploit the mediumship of tree roots to push through
The humidity and tenebrosity in the depths of the strata
And communicate with each other about the history
Of the thirst of all things on Earth
And about the completely different procreation principles
And behavior patterns of dragons and worms

A tree is a ladle penetrating through the super penetralium in the strata
To directly extract freshwater from seawater
And is a blue kid holding the ladle handle of the Big Dipper
Scooping impossible spring water and dark clouds from the depths
        of constellations
And enabling horses, camels and almost burning deserts to drink water
A tree lets the idle chatter of the sky and tree leaves
Rest in bird nests as if resting in cradles
Like the blue kid chasing his homeland's clouds
And when exhausted   like a blue worm   swinging back and forth
While hanging on his homeland's tree leaves

The man cutting down trees   the man overtly claiming that
The felling of the trees is to clear the way for high-voltage power lines
And to drive away mosquitoes and birds defecating in yards
The man having separated a big room into two small chambers
Insulated one of the chambers into a darkroom
Conspiring in the darkroom and commanding the felling process
The man hidden behind the forever tightly closed darkroom curtains
Observing and counting the urban residents impeding the felling project
Identifying them one by one and having created a corresponding blacklist
The man hewing the trees until they look like
Punitively tattooed people with limbs hacked off

Holding up their ghastly wounds resembling broken necks in broad daylight
As if wailing silently
The man with crisscross folds and ridges in his occipital area
That look like a heap of intertwining venomous snakes
The man resembling one who subsists by chewing excrement for a lifetime
Will definitely look uglier than a worm if he dies
Even if he has settled down next to a funeral home
And started learning to mingle with black dust, dung and dirt a long
        time ago
If he dies he will look like a worm or a dead dog
No one will be willing to claim his body for burial
He won't be accepted to his ancestral graveyard covered by thorns instead
        of trees
Or to the funeral home where stinking dark fumes curl up every day
He is doomed to die without a burial place

The Mediterranean Sea

Today I want to write about the Mediterranean Sea
The sea where several more refugee ships capsized
Where many more women   children and brooding-eyed men
Were dumped like rotten fish and shrimps to feed the shoals

Among all the oceans in the world   the Mediterranean is most famous
It's an ocean that holds the lyre of the blind poet Homer
And the esoterica about Poseidon, god of the sea
Combating against the sea, above the endlessly roaring waves
All the oceans in the world contain death   deep abysses
And Lethean water that will lead astray the souls of the dead
Since the Mediterranean started at the era when the gods chased each other
Bronze and rocks have been polishing the ancient beach
Those scorched by fire and immersed by floods in their homeland
Those ships and people having veered off their homeland as if defecting
Today are sedimented on the seabed with piles of their corpses
Neither warships nor planes would see their smallness and desperation again

Today the Mediterranean Sea I am writing about
Is a tomb inside time
Europe's blood   and a bowl of cold blood that has knocked out
The incisors of Homer, of the gods and of time

Different Forms of Mourning

On the leas of the Mu Us Desert
At many places the desert is low   so are the hills
The herbs and shrubs are lower than the hillocks
With some curls that can only be rendered by mourning
Some of them look like pot lids   growing flat
Others are like inverted woks
Clinging tightly to the sand dunes and growing downwards

On the Mu Us Desert   birds and the setting sun
Together are slowly flying into the distance
A very rare horse   when spotted by chance
Is towering in the sunset like a bronze statue
An azure blue lake   when noticed occasionally
Performs so unexpectedly and restlessly
Just like the tear relic accidentally shed by an alien mourner

Humble Sea-Watcher

Swarmed on the beach were sea-watchers
Seafowl too were flocking on a reef afar
While the sea-lookers were watching the ocean
The birds were hiding from and also watching them
While timely tidying the weariness and messiness
Rendered by winds and clouds to their feathers and wings
Shortly after their return from the ocean voyage
I was jostled by the crowd to the last row
At that disadvantaged place   I could still see
The first giant roaring bubbles smelly of the sea
Rushed up to the beach
I was afraid of those bubbles
And the people shouting with bubbles in arms
I was originally intending to meet genuine seawater
Briny seawater   even if it with fangs
Would bite me cruelly   until bleeding
Until exposing of glistening white bones
However witnessing the giant bubbles and screaming crowd
Isolate the real seawater
I only wanted to take some steps back further
To a far place without the uproar of the bubbles and crowd
I only wanted to listen in the quietude to know
If there was an ocean
Not anywhere else
But growling inside me

The Reason I Like Glass

What I like about glass
Is its numerous acute angles
Sharper than knives but never engaged in killing
What I like about shattered glass
Is the acute angles represented by each bit of broken glass
And immeasurable even with the aid of a flat plane
What I like about the cracks on shattered glass
Is the cracks of the indeterminable acute angles
Borne by the principle of brewing lightning by thunderheads
And only controllable by the person
Catching lightning with bare hands
And regarding the capture as beauty
Just like controlling flowers and plants

III

All the World's Birds Are
Flying Towards Twilight

.

All the World's Birds Are Flying Towards Twilight

All the world's cities are expanding towards the suburbs
All the world's birds are flying towards the dusk over the outskirts
The peach blossom pond there fortunately encircled by a bamboo grove
And the moors luckily shrouded by denser woods
Are the places where all the world's birds
Choose to meet their relatives and kins at dusk

The verdant woods and bamboo grove
Occupy a large expanse of cropland and the village's abandoned land
As places that have driven away a large number of people and households
And desolate areas half mantled and half decorated by woods
Incalculable shadowy birds   like numerous shards of darkness
Blot out the sky and cover up the ground while flying towards here at dusk
They are effervescing in the gloomy dimness unique to the suburbs
                and woods
As if they were going to launch an insurgence

All the world's birds are flying in the twilight
Towards the suburbs firmly occupied by the woods and bamboo forest
Where there is neither a pagoda spire for the birds to intertwine
Nor the moon for them to linger and twirl around
The giant flock of birds seems to have just woken up
And seems to awake all the desolation and bleakness
Of the entire suburbs, the entire woods
And their entire wilderness in the darkness
To take them to another place

On a Sinner-Like Wasteland

All the world's good lands have become suburbs today
All the world's suburbs   places that are just a breath away
Far places   strange places
All have a sinner-like wasteland today
There, the old wood stump covered with jelly ears and crowded around
        by weeds
Wheat growing with the weeds and thriving into barnyard grass
Corn, soybean and sorghum that grow tall but don't produce ears or pods
Is as lonely as an exile with only its shadow as its company
And looks so self-abased as if it couldn't be less inferior
What if a person bobs up suddenly in the wasteland
And crops up like a ghost without any reason
He looks left and right like a fugitive and can't withhold
His panicky feeling as if mistakenly trespassing a forbidden place
Eager to cross through towards the end of the wilderness
He treads down a large area of weeds as if overwhelming rivals
And also tramps out all the inferiority complex of the barnyard grass
That seems to be kidnapped to another place

In the center of the great sinner-like wasteland
Even the sinner escaping to another place intends not to stay
The weeds and barnyard grass tramped and conquered by him
Beat from the back just like rebels
His way to escape
That is guided by the slow and fluctuating flight
Of a bird having almost lost the ability to fly
And that leads to alps afar shrouded by misty clouds
And to the silent horizon

All the world's good lands have become suburbs today
Even the quiet raptors living on the crags in remote valleys
And the stars seeming to be at one's fingertips like insect chirps
Are part of the sinner-like wasteland and therefore
Have sinner-like gaze   bright yet dazed

Observation of a Flying Flamingo

A flamingo weeping in the skies
Must have fallen behind in a flight accident
Having lost all its companies
It's flying alone in its own weeps

Just like me at this moment
A person loving to walk solo
Alone in the distance   due to my sensitivity
Due to the lonesome walk in the lengthy valley shadows
I am startled by the sobs of the flamingo
Thus I look up for a long, long time
At the flamingo and its fiery arduous flight
Even my heart indulges into flaming hot befuddlement
Like the shadow beset by the scorching sun on a lofty bluff
Shivering imperceptibly
And like a blade hiding in the shades of a heap of silk
Wriggling as if shuddering

The flamingo is weeping in the skies
Such a lonely flamingo inadvertently falling behind
Is depleting itself in its burning red lonesome flight
Towards a distant perch in an anonymous ocean

Or it will let its own flight
Together with its scorching red body
Haunted by more and more vertigo due to excessive flight
On its halfway   not fall naturally
But plummet as if in an accident
On the depths of an anonymous ocean

Curved Scenery

All the trees here are born to be curved
Just like question marks with a birth defect
All the winds here are curved as well
The horizon with rolling gloomy clouds
Is the place where they crookedly crisscross
Nevertheless the winds here are massive
Like a kind of strength carving the world in nihility
With the dimensions of the sky and the beauty of emptiness
The bird that is testing the winds
And trying to descend from the sky to get close to the ground
Is blown to a higher place by a random gale
Its slanted flight with unsteady posture
And the stagger and tilt of a desert trekker
Seem to overlap with each other possibly anytime
But always maintain a distance that can only be clarified
By the sky and the winds

Firmament by the Bell Tower

The firmament alongside the Bell Tower
Gave a feeling of low-slung occlusion at nightfall
A cloud and a bird skimmed low together with sparse raindrops
Not having diverted timely   some part of them inadvertently
Crashed into the tower and its lofty pinnacle concurrently

The crunch of the raindrops and the squeak of the bird
Fell on the ground almost simultaneously
I witnessed this shocking scene   and another scene
Of the ruptured cloud's free gravity and consequent faint vague dimness
As well as some other overanxious green leaves
And the listless languid blossoms burgeoning in the square park
That were all infatuated by this damp dimness

Dark clouds and rain continuously descended and started to destroy
A young married woman in love and the rouge on her cheeks
And as a decoration, the breasts she had tried to augment with sponges
Compared to the pinnacle of the tower pointing to the sky
Compared to a natatorium pool and a fish pond
Compared to the backs of the swimmers and the fish goblins
They are more difficult to delineate and delimit
And harder to apply exact criteria to

Marmot Singing in the Morning Glow

The cart of the morning glow rumbles   its advantage is
Even a marmot can wake up much earlier
Much earlier than humans
Like a standing commander in the morning
The marmot is singing at a lofty place of the universe
Singing on the Qin Mountains

I live in the suburbs   on an expanse of tableland
Haply left by two rivers wrestling together
A place where I can overlook the Qin Mountains
I also awaken with the cart of the morning glow
Sometimes I wake up even earlier than it
I stroll alone and look to the other shore in solitude
A man who practices singing by the running water
Is singing in the morning in my place

Mary's Blizzard and Boy

Gentle Mary   the entire winter is a stiff blizzard
In the snow squall you are accompanying a pale little boy
Who knows how to play games with the snow blast
Builds big snowmen continuously   and uses much red paper
To make big chili-red noses for many giant snowmen
When he ignores the presence of all the other people
And falls into his concentration and silence
The storm becomes piercingly cold and pure

Gentle Mary   secret Mary
The pale boy has played too much in the snowfall
Snow white and bloody red   his snow architecture
Has rendered her a surprising sight
Of the nunly quietude of the entire winter snow
And the hardly controllable secret enchanting charm
Concealed in this nun-like snowscape
And starting inside her body   like surging tides

Gentle Mary   in the depths of the winter's snow scene
Can't help accompanying it as fresh as a lotus root
Your lips have surged like the torrents of spring
Regardless of those arriving snow watchers
You will dash out recklessly   or in the world's bowels
Shout alone the name of the quiet pale boy
The names of the giant snowmen with big chili-red noses

And shout to what is as reserved as the snow landscape in the internal world
What is sleeping soundly on a winter night in the depths of a blizzard
What she seems unable to wake up again by herself
The snowscape, which belongs to a boy
And also to herself

Python of Time

Like a river
The python of time entangles itself with water
Until the water becomes calm yet unfathomable
Meanwhile like a riverbed and a grand canyon
It entwines and thrashes the entire river
And twines the giant boulders
That have filtered out not only all the sand but also all the classics
And have thus become more thickheaded   more ancient than the riverbed
But are unfortunately clustered around and fettered
By tourists' trash and waste like tattered batting

With a tree and a big river's
Serenity like that of abandoned ruins
And even with the miraculous obsession
Of an outlander with an unfamiliar desolate place
The python of time
Entwines the mountains with its hollow valleys
Occasionally it lies on a wildland conquered and then deserted
While winding the horizon with its smoke signals [1]
That have wolf eyebrows and eyes

If you are fond of dreaming
And love to waste a lot of time in dreams
Its long waist as giant as a cable
Will crane into the window now and then in your dreams

[1] Smoke signals (狼烟; pinyin: láng yān) refer to the smoke from the wolf dung burnt to signal warfare in ancient China.

Portrait: Sketch of Another Tree

The tree's fruits are stars
Its nest is the universe with stars
Floating like isles in the infinite blue

Its dragonlike roots entwine
A planet called Earth
Oh its massive roots   are soaring on Earth
In the ocean and in its boundless blue
In the vast ground and in its skeleton called stones

The weight of this entire planet
The weight of this aged planet called Earth
Including its fatal lightness in the universe
Comparable to the lightness of a balloon
It is soaring together with all of them

From wind to wind
From the mundane world to beyond
The tree is soaring in the air
And winging in the universe
Like a bird not hatching eggs
But incubating a galaxy of stars
The flying tree   is ceaselessly brooding
The lonely flight
Of the bird of eternity
Resounding through the serene universe

A Fish Controlled by an Accidental Ideal

As a fish living in a river
I have lived for so long   tired of living
Now I want to become a fish living and making air bubbles
Inside your body and breath

Just like a kind of unmatchable fictional beauty
It's a project vaster than the ocean since the ocean came into being
I will choose to gently enter you during intervals of your breath
Will continuously circumvent your breath
To avoid the misfortune of being spat out by you
Will clean the crescent moon and shattered glass out of your system
To remove like detoxication their periodically relapsing blades
And will secretly carry out work in the dark like an undercover agent

At the time when you breathe I will lurk deeper
I will hold my breath   or burst into howl
A kind of howl like from a beast gleaming with green light
It can greatly subdue the pain   and help you maintain proper balance
During the continuous penetration of my ideal-controlled body
It is inevitable that you and I are to suffer the torture of an ideal
And to constantly savor the beauty of changes or anguish
Just as the structure of your body will be destroyed
And your body temperature will soar crazily as if enchanted
Which will be a kind of test and trial to my scales
Black scales   will be diluted by the slow heat
Or will be gradually stewed into mysterious brownish red
They will incessantly swell   become plump and enormous
And turn into something with a heavy fishy smell   more controllable
Easier to capture   so that I can hand them over without reservation
And entrust them to you as if entrusting my afterlife

Friction is inevitable   just like gradual retreat into the dreamland
It is a kind of blessed beauty to die from slow asphyxiation in the dreamworld
The process of entry witnesses the successive disappearance of all the parts of self

But I am astounded by my presence at more places inside you
The old me is only a fabricated imaginary self
I am your puppet   symbol and metaphor
Only when returning to your body   with all parts disintegrated
Can I remove my armor and show my true colors
And become a happy baby   as immaculately clean as a fish
Eventually I will transform into a pearl inside your body
To light you up   so that you can finally see yourself
It is your existence that can only be seen by yourself
An intangible existence

I am a fish that has entered your body
When I   and all the beauty I have experienced
But don't have time to narrate   disappear in your body
Only you will know I am a fish having experienced many vicissitudes
Just like you will repeatedly dream of the way you look from now on
I am still a fish confined in a stone for many years
A fish accidentally from a roe lost on a tree
A fish lingering in a grand canyon and its shadows
A fish sipping from the desert like sipping spring water
A fish surviving the disaster of being hit by a fallen star
It once traversed the sand beach on which it was stranded
And even fled a tree just like a ripe fruit
Since circumstances change with the passage of time, it has found
Its own river   the river of clouds
The river of birds and the moon river

I am a fish living in an unknown river
Now this river is inside your body
It has vanished into thin air but is ubiquitous just like me
I am familiar with this river   just like with myself
And also understand today's you   such as you never like greed
I no longer like super-wide things
Such as the ocean   such as the firmament hanging over my head
Like an ocean but wider than an ocean, and its broader blue
I am fed up with the pursuit in which I am tied up with a river
Instead I choose your body   enter your body

Dissolve in your body like a secret agent loving to tap into terra incognita
Transform your body into a river
And disappear myself completely in the river   as if I had never existed
So that when you disappear
I can still exist inside you
This sense of existence is another state of your being
Both you and I seem to lurk in eternity

I am a fictional imaginary fish living in a river
It is a necessity for me to escape the fabrication
In order to transform into a real fish living inside your body
I must alter my shape   and master the stealth technique in the air
Now in this dragging project like overturning the ocean
Each step is more inconceivable than the last
Tree roots grow invertedly and water is about to flow reversely
Rivers run towards the North and mountains are going to collapse
Who can exercise sound judgment
It's very difficult to enter you   just like darkness entering light
To conceal itself well

Just like entering death   entering hatred
And entering a bottle of poison that would seal as soon as I enter
It will be a kind of very painful beauty
A method to maintain nihility and to conquer nihility
Exists right after my going through fire and water

What's beyond life and death is the real destination

Heavier or Lighter: Fall of Butterfly or Airplane

While mating on a wild flower
A pair of butterflies struggle and pulsate so much
That they unfortunately fall on the ground   breaking
Their scallop-patterned wings and waists

The jubilant scene embodying secret tendencies
In which the injury is really very severe
Is just like a Boeing 747 diving headlong
Into the Pacific Ocean
And just like a bird flying to a dead end of the firmament
With broken wings on a journey towards ruin
And then handing over together
Its demise and lightness in a gale
To a dark and desperate descent
Over the Pacific Ocean

A pair of colorful butterflies destroyed by falling
The falling of a plane and of a bird
It's not important as to which is lighter or heavier
The most important is that they all
Indiscriminately bind together death and love
And let them fall in a *laissez-faire* way

Fruits Flying Towards All Corners of the World Like Birds

A singular tree   has borne too many fruits
Those ripe fruits are like birds
Flying downwards under the tree in clusters and flocks
Towards afar   towards trains
Along a river until arriving in the ocean
Voyaging at sea on a giant ocean-goer
On and on, they cross the blue as deep
And profound as the ocean and skies
Rushing to the four corners of the world with navigators

Ripe fruits   with more love for their homeland and motherland
And controlled by their dreams to fly
Like birds   harness the wind during flight
And touch down, in swarms and flocks like birds
In the North   in the South
And in the depths of the land as broad as Mother

The fruits with deep love for flight and the horizon like birds
Are continuously landing towards the land's depths
Everywhere on the earth   they assume the posture
Of a bird at its flight intervals
To stay together with stones
To stay together with woods and their cool shades
To stay together with the arched dark backs of cultivators
And to stay together with the gloomy roots in the earth's bowels

The fruits with deep love for flight and the horizon like birds
Adore the landing towards the gloomy roots of the earth
Like a blood transfusionist   from bottom to top
With the quality of transforming fruit into soil   its love
Is deeply grieved   and is also the love of flying

A reserved tree
Well versed in the principle "high as heaven and deep as the earth"

That regenerates each passing day
Has borne too many fruits
Succulent fruits   encapsulate full plump seeds
Like flocks within flocks of birds
And like a flight that contains an unfathomable

Flight

Leaves Fluttering Down Profusely Under the Starry Sky

Leaves do not descend from the starry sky
But from the trees under the stars
At dead of night   the stars are more far-reaching
Through a window of a café
I behold, under an erotically yellow and indolent light
Leaves, like birds shot by a tranquilizer gun
Fall profusely and disorderly

They are striking a sanitation worker in a yellow vest
Who always in the late of night
Indulges in sweeping the light all over the street
And the waste pressed to the bottom of the light
From the dump trucks entering the city
Under the cover of the darkness
Regardless of the overcast sky   that seems to snow
And also hesitate about whether or not it should snow

Regardless of the leaves swirling all over the street
Like plummeting birds

The Man Always Walking Ahead

A man who has controlled his skeletal proportion
And walking posture by music
And who has digested salt into brine in his body
Thereby rendering his tactile system
Keener than an awl and a knife
Is always walking ahead of me

From my long-time observations
The man having kept walking ahead of me
Kept walking in the same direction as I
And perplexed me many times in life
Is also a free man   a wayward man
Who doesn't take the high road under many situations
Many times   when he is dawdling
In the wild barren land ahead
I very much want to stop him by talking to him
Find a boulder, on which to sit with him, and chitchat for a while
However I only go with the stream chasing after him
A man having kept walking towards the seashore
I have chased after him for a lifetime
Until I realize that I am merely his shadow
Whilst he is another shadow of me

It's a man having ignored or suppressed much life's content
And always persisted in walking ahead
A man having digested salt into seawater to propel himself
A man regarding earthly things   as trifles
He only aspires that the day will eventually come
When at the remotest corners of the globe
His internal seawater could collide with the ocean
And chafe out an unknown festering sore

He will grasp a handful of sparkles and festering pains
On the Lofty Stony Mountain on the eastern shore [1]

Like a desperate sea nymph or sea ghost
Intonating incessantly in a slow deep tone

[1] This sentence is translated from the poem "View of the Sea" (观沧海; pinyin: guān cāng hǎi) written by Cao Cao (曹操; pinyin: cáo cāo), a warlord and the penultimate Chancellor of the Eastern Han dynasty who rose to great power in the final years of the dynasty. Lofty Stony Mountain is a translation of Jieshi Mountain (碣石山; pinyin: jié shí shān).

Woman in Exotic Dress

You are a woman fond of exotic dress   with paths beyond paths
Constantly highlighted by the sun and smog
You walk far ahead   hesitant yet firm
Keeping me from following too close   or too far behind
Assured that I have been enticed
I still willingly follow at your heels to the wild

In the legendary grand Central Shaanxi Plain   the legendary basin
Confined by the boulders of Mount Hua and the Qin Mountains
The basin flowing with honey   which has drowned
Dynasties, one after another, in fame, fortune, frivolity and fascination
The basin abundant with rumors by many emperors for your sake
The basin in the ripening season   with impassive clusters
Of wheat ears and pomegranate fruits
Turning outwards like the labia of a woman about to deliver

The basin as mysterious as the womb of a woman
You cross it unhurriedly   totally oblivious to it
The men having started stalking you secretly in dreams
And been twisted around your little finger as if bewitched
Are outstripped by you a long way
And thus have to start out again in one dream after another
So as to follow hard on your heels

You are a woman fond of odd dress as much as pranks
A woman like not only a fox but also a sprite
You control men's mind
Like mastering the principle of using a magic mirror
Having thrown off so many superficially specious stalkers
You lead me whom you have no way to throw off eventually
To a wilderness that couldn't be any wilder
Use a high green weeping willow beyond reach
To tie me tight   and beat me while you wear a veil
Because I would in no way turn back   you forcibly tear

Your veil and constrict my neck   while threatening
Again and again to strangle and break my neck

You are a woman having meticulously dressed up
And tempered bizarre dress into something as sharp and ethereal as a soul
Your savagery that regards romance as beauty is invincible
Your followers have followed you wave after wave
Before you and also after you
I am the only persister and outlaster   destined to
Take pride in the obsession with quest of you in your wilderness
Day and night

Peace-Minded Man by the Salween River

On a giant boulder by the Salween River
The man with a mind as tranquil as still water
Sometimes sits about for the whole day
Sometimes plays ducks and drakes all day long
On the raging billows of summer's Salween River
On the raging orange billows on a summer morning
On the raging saffron billows on a summer high noon
On the raging jade billows under summer's starlight
Sometimes mounts a sky-high mountain like a beast
Pushes boulders in a tottering position down the cliff
Watches them beat down a row of indignant turbid waves
And get another row of turbid waves
Taller and more indignant, to bounce up immediately like beasts
And witnesses the black giant boulders
Cutting through the turbid waves
As if crossing through a pack of routed wolves
And then sinking gradually into the middle of the river
After momentary rolling and undulation

The peace-minded man by the Salween River
Is a man with time hanging heavy on his hands
A man of unknown origin and as erratic as a shadow
A man who sometimes emerges and other times disappears
Leaving no trace behind

Ennui

Fed up with the park's stones
Trees with growth curbed by I.V. bottles
Apartments   vehicles' exhaust fumes   smog
As well as the magnificence and luxury of the downtown
That hides its dumping ground, flies and mosquitoes
In a wilderness as if it were hiding thieves

Between our city and the next
I am tired of sailing out on the ocean
With the mediocre helmsman
The brine clusters the isles enveloped in despair
The birds following the liner actually are only
Chasing after the trash in the hands of sea players
And the curve of sludge and turbid water in the blue
That is drawn by the vomit-like excrement
Discharged by the sewage system, larger than the mast, in the liner
Throughout the entire voyage

I am weary of all these filthy, mercilessly pestering things
As a man who has a slightly dejected mind
And sometimes can't help getting angry
I just want to go to the farthest place alone
A place only a liner or an aircraft
Pushing the limits of its strength could reach
I just want to jump into the ocean with a meteorite
Burn with it together in the ocean
Or stay alone with the empty city like nirvana

Horizon Bent by Gloomy Clouds Part I

More and more damp south winds traverse Mount Tai each day
With some kind of heavily misty sweetness and fierceness
That can only be controlled by the vault of heaven
And with the gloomy clouds fluttering towards here from the ocean
Like wallowing whales, and chasing after my lover like a fairy

Humid dark clouds   waterlogged dark clouds
Gloomy clouds allover the sky resembling teetering water bags or breasts
With some kind of sweet fleeciness that can control the celestial dome
Are chasing after my lover who, once strong-willed
Even looks down upon emperors and people of extreme power
They press down continuously   the ground becomes low   a close-up view
The entire celestial arc and the entire world seeming to be pushed
To the verge of collapse   are girding up their loins
And restlessly gestating another kind of gush
More dangerous than the gushing of the dark clouds

The gloomy clouds and winds have bent
The treetops in the plain and its horizon afar
Power lines cutting through the sky as if cutting through a belly
And unhurried chimes resonating above the Bell Tower in the city hall square
A skylark having strayed into the city and trying to fly in a straight line
Has to continuously escape from the dark clouds and its own falling
Has to surprisingly bypass those unexpected power lines
And therefore its flight has become a curved yet dangerous art

Dark damp clouds and winds are flying angrily in the North
On the northern mountains that seem to totter and collapse
On the horizon of the North
Above the head of my lover yelling at me to chase the clouds
And over the head of mine while I was chasing my lover with clamors

The gloomy clouds and I are chasing after my lover together
The person speedier and more willful than the dark clouds and winds

If my lover runs too fast
And inadvertently bumps into the horizon bent by the gloomy clouds
I will immediately follow her and dash forward   till lightning bursts out
Or the gloomy clouds and horizon perish secretly

My lover and I will collide together
And like the bird rolling and tumbling in the dark clouds
Will transform not only ourselves
But also the entire world   at the moment of collision
Into a curved yet dangerous art
That even belittles the horizon

Horizon Bent by Gloomy Clouds Part II

Damp winds and moist dark clouds from the ocean
Wake up together with my heart and this spring
My lover with hair dyed redder than fire
Who loves to lie in, awakens too

The damp winds are unrestrainedly blowing my lover
Fond of strolling around the streets alone
The blow has opened her collar and exposed
Her neck and chest so fair as to suffocate an onlooker
As well as her cleavage as stingy as lightning
She heartily likes me to spy upon and observe her secretly
When I pretend to meet her on the street by chance

Oh my dear lady   my dear little fairy
Has already started to perform her lethal tricks
She doesn't know her attractive breasts and buttocks
Are like two bags of dynamite embedded in my fate
That have lurked in my body since my previous life
At the moment when I can no longer suppress myself
They have already started to undulate vehemently
Inside the firmament and my breath
Just like the gloomy clouds continuously falling
And crashing under the blow of the wind
Now they are being torn apart stealthily piece by piece
And are awakening secretly   with a thirst for sprinting
Like wings starting to spread infinitely enormous
And like the fuse of a dynamite having been kindled
Hissing and fizzing

The gloomy clouds have bent the horizon
The ground thus becomes lower and lower
My darling   a lady never wary of me
The fairness of her fair chest and fair neck
As well as the cuteness of her breasts and buttocks

Are becoming more and more unbridled
Because of my choice to walk together with her
As if they wanted me to draw gently near
The lethal moment under the dark clouds

I am enduring cruel excruciation
My lover is spraying poison   like abandoning yellow dust
The honey intensively clustered in her pistils like a hive
And the sweet poisonous thorns from her dense stems
Are hurled around by her in large bundles just like a snowscape
They, each more lethal than the last, are stacked in my heart

After the damp winds and dark clouds from the ocean
My lover, in an occasional fit of pique and bad temper
Is running   forcing me to start chasing
The reckless pursuit awakes during the onset of the toxicity
We, both out of control and shouting, run through spring

This impetuous, custom-made spring awakes from sleep too
The stop-and-go lady playing games with the clouds and winds
As a hunter   recklessly pursues and competes
In the knockout gradually carried out between two people
By her who is holding a kite
An extremely dangerous match against the clouds and winds
She doesn't exclude herself
Nor the possible death

I must forget about myself   and become a monster
So must my darling   we pretend that
We are fighting with the winds and dark clouds
My lover has red nails more coquettish than a fairy's
And all the hauteur as if she could easily control time
As well as thin, long palms   the only way out
Is to give up outsmarting   like a giant python
Subduing its murderous look while gradually curling up
Or like an infant domesticated by a beast of prey

I am infatuated with all these things   or maybe
Before the battle and match end   I will choose
On my own initiative to fail in my lover's hands
I will be most willing to choose to give up and die
Falling slowly with saliva dripping down
Just like a fun-loving child who, tired of playing
Is soundly falling into Morpheus's slumberland

The slumber sweeter and deeper than poison
Is grasped so tightly by my lover's thin, long palms
I wish it, like a loose-fitting sleeping bag
Would become looser and looser

As if the gloomy clouds had bent the horizon

History of Clouds

Clouds' white furry-fuzzy belly
Has returned to the home of Sister Moon
Their red, sedate yet showy belly
Has returned to the home of Brother Sun

Their dark belly
As dark as iron   as dark as black lacquer
A little bit above the treetops of the forest
With the curvature as curving and furious as lightning
Has shoveled through ferociously like a shovel loader
And hewed down expanses of black forests
One after another

Thereafter, the dark-bellied clouds wobbly and totteringly
Hide in a tuft of grass having survived on the mountaintop
With part of them hiding
In the burrow of a marmot on the mountainside
And in a palace hidden more deeply than Grandpa's Grandpa
More exquisite, kind-hearted and weaker than a fairy tale
A palace made of the crystals from a mountain ghost

Varieties of clouds
(Are actually the same kind of clouds)
In various directions
Are chasing after each other   fleeting and flitting

The clouds of this year   and the clouds of last year
Are all clouds
But with totally different sugar content
Oxygen content   iron content   and electric charges

Red Fox: A Legend

Coquettish like a legendary red fox
That has mastered many sets of enticing tricks
And crisscrossed the Zhongnan Mountains afar
Hidden and nurtured in my heart is a good girl
If you want to have the luck to meet her
It's not that easy

The world's best peaks are hidden in the Qin Mountains
The world's number one peaks are the Zhongnan Mountains
On those heights as deep and recondite as secrets
There is an increasing number of travelers
And an increasing number of people for the secrets
Even though too many people can jeopardize things
Even though the more people, the more interfering eyes
Oh, such a good girl
Is like a startling red fox setting the world on fire
Unless you are extremely fortunate
It's not that easy for you to meet her

You can imagine that she lives in the Zhongnan Mountains
With the risk and danger of your imagination lying in that
As a person with secrets hidden in your heart
Everything in the mortal world   you'll gradually abandon
And start to turn to questing secrets   turning out
You become bogged down deeper and deeper in the secrets
Burrow through the mountains more and more deeply
And will disappear in the Zhongnan Mountains
Earlier than she   earlier than the good girl like a red fox

You will leave or stray much earlier than she
And in the name of the Zhongnan Mountains
(But not the growing number of travelers
With plastic bags and scouting instruments)
Will disappear without a trace from now on

Four Birds at the Watershed Between the River and the Ocean

A stormy petrel is winging in chase of billows and hilsa herring
An albatross is sailing in chase of a giant liner about to be launched
And its mourning sirens
An anonymous bird is soaring   resembling a red-crowned crane
Stretching its long neck and legs in the sky
While at the starting point of the ocean   in a shipyard
On a scaling ladder attached to a ten-thousand tonner
Having just finished the last process for an oceangoing voyage
An elated mechanic accidentally losing his footing
Is flying like a bird towards the ocean and his death

A Girl Talking With a Mirror

The girl astray for long in the moors and shadows
Ending up dashing back home luckily and suddenly
Nurtures a mirror in a dark room
Wrapped with a piece of black silk
Gently lifting up the black silk in the dark
By the gloomy light dimmer than a soul inside the mirror
She is pouring her heart out alone

In a dialogue with herself in and with the mirror
With the gloomy light of her soul hidden inside black curtains
And her face scrubbed to be smoother
And more elusive than the mirror
The girl always wants to know her own family origin
And the lowdown hung in the mirror, deeper than the curtains
And to acquire a special sleeping skill

She always wants to return to the mirror like in a dream
To sleep stark naked in the mirror
Like a mirror   like a nude

Porcelain Cleaner in a Gloomy Apartment

She must clean something every day
The rouge and powder on her face   some odds and ends
That her pants are somehow inadvertently stained with
And that are used for cleaning herself
She uses a large bucket of shoddy detergent
To clean, over and over, the porcelain toilet
Tirelessly splashes water to cleanse the porcelain floor
Utilizes a dentiform violentish cast iron brush
To strenuously scrub all the porcelains in the apartment
Until they are deeply scratched and scraped
Until the violent cast iron brush
Seems to cut deeply into herself
Hurting herself

Talking About Snow With a Girl in a Café

The imperceptible flush of rose hidden in the fairness
Of the girl's face fairer than a lotus flower
Enabled me to completely forget the winter outside

The girl always seemed to deliberately avoid
Discussions about the winter
However eventually   she talked about the snow

I took a look through the window of the café
The trees were indeed nearly divested of foliage
A sanitation worker regarding all her geese as swans
With a broomstick in her hands
Was staring blankly at the lights allover the street
And hunkering down to handle the ground from time to time
Just like a patient yet sensitive hen
Looking for the deeply buried seeds or worms

Silence. Melancholy light. On the microwave
A reheated coffee pot was hissing with steam
And occasional slight gulping sounds of swallowing.

Like a topic gradually approaching the verge of danger   that girl
Slowed down her speech   never mentioned snow again
I too became evasive   and shifted the topic to another
——It was because it had already started to snow outside

I felt the snow falling so urgently   yet so nicely
Like that girl's face fairer than a lotus flower
In the disturbing susurration of the snow
The world was slowly turning white

Man With a Nose As Huge as a Spacecraft

The man with a nose as huge as a spacecraft
Lives in the same alley as I   experiences together with me
The bird droppings gravitating from the leaves at a high place
The roads with pets' excrement and urine to be seen everywhere
And the bizarre gaze contained in the eyes of other people
I remember his simple, tolerant and forgiving smile

His big nose so lofty as to be nearly exaggerated
Yet still so appropriate and decent
Renders his arms and palms slander and elongated
As a highly sensitive man   I always take it for granted that
This appearance will definitely hinder him from becoming a man
Who hunkers head-down while working for a living
But actually he is a longshoreman working on a nearby dock
Loading cargo during the daytime
Watching over departing vessels at night
And raising a colony of injured seabirds
He has salvaged from the seashore, in his free time

The man with a nose as huge as a spacecraft
Magnificent physique   heavy weight   and big strides
Goes to work early and comes back late in our alley like a giant bird
Sometimes you can't find any sign of him
Or have any information about his ride
On a ship out to the ocean to another place

I hypothesize that he must have spent some time on flight
Only that he is like those seabirds he nurtures
Who heal their internal injuries in a dark place   once recovered
Love to fly on a cliff   on trees   or on a mast
And can be rarely beheld by ordinary people

The Place I Want to Go

The place I want to go
Is the place even a mountain   or a river wants to go
The place a worm or a squirm of worms want to go
To produce silk, spin cocoons and transition to moths and butterflies
The place where the moon keeps itself aloof from the firmament
And tries its best to lean against the hilltop and treetops
The place where a squirrel coming down from a tree depleted of food
Can find long-awaited fruits and a large heap of grass seeds
The place where a stone, like a bear losing its footing
While crossing the river, embosoms the riverbed and more smaller stones
And sleeps soundly in a valley with birds flying over occasionally
And in its shadows

The place I want to go
Is the place where an emperor inelegantly has his imperial robe wetted
              by dews
Where a living person aspires to go to dream
And a dead body wants to go to lay its white bones
Where the blank time itself, deserted by the bee of time
Which has inadvertently lost its poisonous stinger as well as honey,
              wants to go
And where time of time itself, the only thing left
Holds a gust of wuthering autumn wind but can't even feel
That it is embracing wobbled, somewhat unsteadily standing, nihility

Seven Lakes and Seven Swans

There are seven swans in seven lakes
Laying eggs
Or aspiring to hatch more swans from the eggs

Only at seven high places, where one can
Almost touch the pure bright blue of the sky,
Can one overlook the seven lakes
With scrubby verdantly lush woods and reeds
And reachable only by passing morasses
Resembling layers of labyrinths

These stretches of mires can even devour a live ox
Driven into it   treacherous yet serene mires
Where only sunshine other than humans can easily enter

In the seven lakes accessible only to swans
Seven swans loving quietude and peace
Nest and lay eggs in lake-blue tussocks
With their curved necks resembling the Big Dipper
Still yet elegant

The seven swans in the seven lakes
Are either laying eggs   or are brooding
The quietude of all the lakes or the entire starry sky
Their tall necks resembling the handle of the Big Dipper
Fade in and out in the dark green of the tussocks
And the dark blue of the lakes
Just like seven stars that don't stint on hiding or running wild

Reasons for Only Reading Friends' Books

This life seems long but actually not
I wish that I could alienate myself from
Reading masterpieces from now on
And only read friends' books

It's only because these friends
Are like swans
Phoenixes
Dragons or tigers
Only dwelling in the depths of clouds
In the belly of woods
And in the bowels of torrential currents
Only I can discriminate their traces
Only I can know their lairs
Only I can identify their voices

Demise of the Starry Sky

The man having seen the demise of the starry sky
Is a man knowing when to accept or reject
A man climbing trees to look for water
A man sailing in the ocean to seek for clouds
A man embracing the dragon neck of a mountain range
To take its body temperature
He knows very well the ins and outs of many things
No matter where he is, it's a place
As far as in the past or in a foreign land

The man having seen the demise of the starry sky
No matter where you are, he will see you
You too are walking alone
Not to seek for something   but for the sake of walking
The massive wilderness and horizon
Are only the background of another person
You have no direction, but only distance
While you become smaller and smaller
As if you were a man with an odd mind-body size
Going to meet another man with an odd mind-body size

The man having seen the demise of the starry sky
Knowing which of the many things in the world
Is more or less, deeper or shallower
Like the palm of his hand
Whom you are going to meet but not sure about
Sees the earth is changing   the earth is plummeting in the earth
He himself is plummeting in the earth as well

Just like looking up at the vault of heaven
Where the enormous stars thinner, tinier
And more fragile than mosquitoes and flies
Slowly burn down
In an incineration difficult to perceive and comprehend
While plummeting towards nihility, one after another

Men Bringing Stones From Afar

The men searching for stones at unknown places
Hunkering over day and night like the Foolish Old Man [1]
While excavating stones at places
Where no stones can be seen
And rap-tapping to search for stones among stones
With unearthed stones in their arms
Are stone workers away from hometown for many years

Oh, stone workers
The men bringing stones from afar
Return from places with no access
To flight, railroad or highway
Come down from untraversed mountains
Come back from unfrequented wilderness
Come home from the ocean-like ruins
Formed by the remains of abandoned ships
And of a lake dried out by a burning meteorite
And return from the curve of the horizon
Where the shards from stars fly hither and thither
Like small insects, igniting the dark with sparkles

They have a reunion with the city after so long
But instead of going home, they go directly
To newly built downtown Ocean Museum Center
And Volcanic Ash Gallery

[1] The Foolish Old Man (愚公; pinyin: yú gōng) is a character portrayed in the Chinese Taoist text *Liezi*, who was determined to move mountains.

Acknowledgements

We, the translators, sincerely thank *River River* for publishing the poem "An Aesthete's Nails and Hammer," *The Festival Review* for publishing the poem "How to Observe Dark Clouds Polish Constellations," *Anomaly* for publishing the poems "A Bare-Handed Lightning Catcher" and "The Man Digging a Well at the Seashore," *Sinking Water Review* (the literary journal of the University of Miami) for publishing the poem "Demise of the Starry Sky," *Waymark Literary Magazine* (the literary journal of Kennesaw State University) for publishing the poems "The Beauty of Confrontation" and "A Man With a Horrible Dent in His Head," *The Los Angeles Review* for publishing the poems "Writing Lyrics for a Rocker at a Subway Passage," "A Man's Knife Glint, Moonlight and Starshine," and "Moorland Is My Friend," *Lunch Ticket Magazine* (a literary and art journal from the MFA community at Antioch University Los Angeles) for publishing the poems "City and Its Underground Worker" and "Blue Boy Smuggling Birds' Nests up the Trees," *Pilgrimage* (the literary journal of the Department of English and Foreign Languages at Colorado State University-Pueblo) for publishing the poems "A Bare-Handed Lightning Catcher," "Rocks Living in a Yonder Homeland," and "Direction of Twilight in Ginkgo Manor," and *EOAGH* for publishing the poems "On a Sinner-Like Wasteland," "Observation of a Flying Flamingo," and "Man With a Nose as Huge as a Spacecraft." They are all published in the USA.

Moreover, we want to extend our gratitude to *Lunch Ticket Magazine* (a literary and art journal from the MFA community at Antioch University Los Angeles) as the set of poems, "The Beauty of Confrontation," "A Man With a Horrible Dent in His Head," and "Writing Lyrics for a Rocker at a Subway Passage" was one of six finalists in the *2020 Gabo Prize for Literature in Translation & Multilingual Texts* and was accepted by *Lunch Ticket* for publication in 2020.

Also, many thanks to Charles Alexander for his role in designing and proofreading *A Naturalist's Manor*.

Bios of the Translators

Chen Du is a Voting Member of American Translators Association and a member of the Translators Association of China with a Master's Degree in Biophysics from Roswell Park Cancer Institute, the State University of New York at Buffalo and a Master's Degree in Radio Physics from the Chinese Academy of Sciences. She revised more than eight chapters of the Chinese translation of the biography of Helen Snow, *Helen Foster Snow: An American Woman in Revolutionary China*. In the United States, her translations have appeared in *Columbia Journal, Lunch Ticket, Pilgrimage, Anomaly*, and elsewhere; her poems have appeared in *Levitate, American Writers Review*, and elsewhere; her essay was published by *The Dead Mule* and *Hamline University English Department*; and her poetry chapbook was published by *The Dead Mule* online. A set of three poems co-translated by her and Xisheng Chen was one of six finalists in the *2020 Gabo Prize for Literature in Translation & Multilingual Texts*. She is also the author of the book *Successful Personal Statements*. Find her online at ofsea.com.

Xisheng Chen, a Chinese American, is an ESL grammarian, lexicologist, linguist, translator, and educator. His educational background includes: top scorer in the English subject in the National College Entrance Examination of Jiangsu Province, a BA and an MA from Fudan University, Shanghai, China (exempted from the National Graduate School Entrance Examination owing to excellent BA test scores), and a Mandarin Healthcare Interpreter Certificate from the City College of San Francisco, CA, USA. His working history includes: translator for Shanghai TV Station, Evening English News, Lecturer at Jiangnan University, Wuxi, China, Adjunct Professor at the Departments of English and Social Sciences of Trine University (formerly Tri-State University), Angola, Indiana, notary public, and contract high-tech translator for Futurewei Technologies, Inc. in Santa Clara, California, USA. As a translator for over three decades, he has published a lot of translations in various fields in newspapers and journals in China and abroad. A set of three poems co-translated by him and Chen Du was one of six finalists in the *2020 Gabo Prize for Literature in Translation & Multilingual Texts*.

Bio of the Poet

Yan An is one of the most famous poets in contemporary China, author of fourteen full-length poetry collections including his most famous poetry collection, *Rock Arrangement*, which has won him The Sixth Lu Xun Literary Prize, one of China's top four literary prizes. As the winner of various national awards and prizes, he is also the Vice President of Shaanxi Writers Association, the head and Executive Editor-in-Chief of the literary journal Yan River, one of the oldest and most famous literary journals in Northwestern China. In addition, he is a member of the Poetry Committee of China Writers Association.

Chax Press

Founded in 1984 in Tucson, Arizona, Chax Press has published more than 240 books in a variety of formats, including handprinted letterpress books and chapbooks, hybrid chapbooks, book arts editions, and trade paperback editions such as the book you are holding. From August 2014 until July 2018 Chax Press resided in the University of Houston-Victoria Center for the Arts. Individual donors have supported *A Naturalist's Manor*. Chax is a nonprofit 501(c)(3) organization which depends on support from various government & private funders, and, primarily, from individual donors and readers. In July 2018 Chax Press returned to Tucson, Arizona. In 2021 Chax Press founder and director Charles Alexander is receiving the Lord Nose Award (named for famed small press pioneer Jonathan Williams of Jargon Books) from the Community of Literary Magazines and Presses, for Lifetime Achievement in literary publishing.

A Naturalist's Manor is the first in what will become a range of books by poets & writers in Shaanxi Province, China. Chax Press wishes to thank the translator Chen Du, the author Yan An, and Hu Zongfeng for making our relationship with Shaanxi writers and translators possible. We also wish to thank Luo Lianggong, Charles Bernstein, and Luo Yimin, for their role in making possible our travels, and many friendships, in China. We consider it a privilege and an honor to be contributing to the relationship of poetry and poetics between the US and China.

Our current address is 1517 North Wilmot Road no. 264, Tucson, Arizona 85712-4410. You can email us at *chaxpress@chax.org*.

You may find CHAX at *https://chax.org*.

You may also find many readings by our authors, as well as our podcasts and other endeavors online on our Chax YouTube channel.

Printed and bound in the United States of America by
McNaughton & Gunn.

Designed by Charles Alexander at Chax Press.
Assistance by Ben Leitner and David Weiss at Chax Press.
Proofreading and other support in the production of this book
comes from Chen Du, of Xi'an, China, and Xisheng Chen, of
Oakland, California, USA.

Display and text type: Adobe Garamond Pro.